a. m.

Stanford

2.2.81

DANCING ON THE BRINK

OF THE WORLD

Dancing on the Brink Of the World

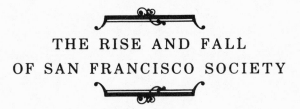

THE RISE AND FALL OF SAN FRANCISCO SOCIETY

Frances Moffat

G. P. PUTNAM'S SONS
NEW YORK

Library of Congress Cataloging in Publication Data
Moffat, Frances.
    Dancing on the brink of the world.
    Includes index.
    1. San Francisco–Social life and customs.
I. Title.
F869.S35M63   1977   979.4′61   77–6894

PRINTED IN THE UNITED STATES OF AMERICA

FOR MY DAUGHTER, GENIE,
AND MY SON, STEPHEN

I am indebted to all who wrote before me, those social historians who clearly perceived the development of San Francisco society. I am grateful for the kindness and cooperation of the Wells Fargo History Room, the libraries of the Mechanics Institute, the California Historical Society and the Society of California Pioneers, and the San Francisco Public Library. I appreciate the fine editing and research assistance of David Siefkin, the patience of John Dodds, senior editor at G. P. Putnam's Sons, and the forbearance of my friends, even those who kept asking, "Whatever happened to that book you were writing?"

Contents

The Costanoan Indians, who lived around San Francisco Bay before the Spanish arrived in 1775, thought, either out of ignorance or wisdom, that they were in a place of great geographic importance. One of their songs began:

"Dancing on the Brink of the World."

1. FANDANGO

As dance after dance was announced and more joined in,
until . . . the whole floor was covered with cotillions
composed entirely of men, with hats on, balancing to
each other, chasséing, everyone heartily enjoying the
exhilarating dance.

McCabe's Journal, 1851.

The American quadrille is danced with Anglo-Saxon
stiffness and impassivity; the Mexican, with southern
languor and indolent grace; but the French quadrille is
the center of genuine gaiety and animation. I often
notice how American men steal away from their own
group and enviously watch.

Albert Benard de Russailh's "Last Adventure, 1851,"
from Julia Altrocchi's *The Spectacular San Franciscans,* 1949.

Late in the afternoon on June 4, 1849, the Pacific Mail
steamship *Panama* sailed through the Golden Gate,
slowed and turned toward the rude wharf at Clark's
Point, below Telegraph Hill. Four hundred passengers
crowded the railing to look at their new city.

The ship glided past a ghostly armada of bare-masted
ships, their hulls rotted and listing, where they had been
abandoned by crews hurrying to get to the gold fields.

Beyond the ships the wharf was crowded and noisy. The din was tremendous; there were men hammering, sacks thudding as they were tossed onto the pier, horses neighing, mules screaming, canvas snapping and voices shouting in a half dozen languages. Above the wharf, a dense brown and white tapestry of canvas awnings, tents and wooden shacks covered the hills. The sky was hazy from the smoke of hundreds of cooking fires.

As the *Panama* docked, Jessie Benton Frémont held up her six-year-old daughter Lily to see their new home. An elegantly dressed young woman, Jessie was the daughter of a United States senator and a member of the most select circle of Washington society. Although she was pale and ill from the long journey, there was no disputing the beauty of her oval face and luminous dark eyes. She had been the first woman to cross the isthmus of Panama on the back of a mule, only to find the steamship *Panama* so crowded that she had to sleep on deck in an iron cot, sheltered by an American flag draped from the boom. Drenched by a rainstorm, she became feverish and was so miserable that a sympathetic passenger gave her his cabin. Now, at last, she was to meet her husband and enter San Francisco society.

Two young men stood near her. One of them, Sam Ward, was conspicuously dressed to fit the illustrious lineage of his pre-revolutionary New York banking family. Among his proud boasts was the fact that his brother-in-law, Adolph Mailliard, was the illegitimate grandson of Napoleon's brother, the one-time king of Naples. He had also been married to Emily Astor until she died in childbirth. He then married the less socially illustrious Medora Grymes, who left him when he inadvertently lost the family fortune in a succession of unfortunate business ventures. His family recommended he begin again in California. His companion, Hall McAllister, was a very young man with a brand-new, unused law degree in his baggage. Neither of them intended to dirty their hands digging for gold; they had safely stowed in the hold of the *Panama* crates of foodstuffs and dry goods to sell.

A tall, craggy-faced, unmistakably Southern gentleman, wearing a carefully tailored suit and carrying an expensive-looking portmanteau, stood near them. This was Dr. William McKendree Gwin. His portmanteau carried letters of introduction to everyone who was supposed to be worth knowing in San Francisco. The letters explained that the bearer was a former Congressman and had once been the confidential secretary to Andrew Jackson. Gwin's ambition in life was to be a United States Senator; Tennessee rejected him, so he chose California.

Finally the landing ramp was lowered to the pier with a crash and the ship made fast. The passengers began the walk into the swarming turmoil of sailors, longshoremen, hotel agents, merchants and teamsters.

Jessie was driven from the wharf by William Davis Merry Howard, a broad-shouldered, prosperous, pre-gold rush pioneer. She and Lily looked around apprehensively as they rode down the street. Each of the wooden shacks lining the street seemed to be a saloon. Groups of men stood about under canvas awnings laughing, arguing and gambling over upended barrels. Where the unpaved street wasn't blocked by wagons, it was clogged by throngs of Chileans in broad sombreros, Chinese with huge baskets and bearded miners in red flannel shirts. From the alleys came the sound of guitars playing fandangos; miners were dancing with one another and staring at Jessie. The whole town looked as if it had been thrown together that afternoon and might be taken down by morning. It was a far cry from the tree-shaded avenues Jessie knew in Washington.

At last they arrived in the center of town where Howard had arranged for Jessie and her daughter to stay. The adobe built by William Leidesdorff, who served as America's vice-consul during the Mexican rule, was furnished in excellent taste. After his death (since he left no heirs), Howard and a group of wealthy businessmen took it over. Jessie relished the luxury of French furniture, fine carpets and the service of a maid while she settled down to await her husband who was, at the moment, riding north from Los Angeles to meet her.

The illegitimate son of a Virginia society belle and a Royalist refugee from the French Revolution, the handsome, dark-bearded Frémont was renowned for his lionlike courage, bearlike tenacity and lemminglike lack of sense. When he was twenty-seven, he married Jessie Benton, the sixteen-year-old daughter of Senator Thomas Hart Benton of Missouri.

In 1846, the government sent Frémont to Yerba Buena, a remote Mexican outpost in California. Several months later, Frémont and his two guides, Kit Carson and Broken-Hand Fitzpatrick, with sixty soldiers, were slogging across the Sierra Nevada Mountains on snow-shoes.

The tiny village of Yerba Buena was happily oblivious of the concern it caused Washington. It had always been an outpost, first of the Spanish Empire when it was founded in 1776, and then, of the shaky Mexican Empire. John Marsh, an American resident, claimed its social life consisted entirely of "getting drunk and running up and down the hills."

This was an oversimplification, of course. In the spring, when the hills by the sea were wreathed in wild strawberries, the whole town pitched tents on the beach where they picnicked and got drunk. In winter, during the rainy season, they gathered indoors to dance the fandango, sing and drink some more. These activities were accompanied by much running up and down the hills.

The social leader here was General Mariano Vallejo who presided over a whitewashed adobe mansion in Sonoma, not far north of Yerba Buena. His father had been a foot soldier with Father Serra on his missionary visit of 1776; his mother was a Lugos from the family that owned a huge rancho in central California. At thirty-nine, Vallejo was a general, with the best library in California, seven daughters, three hundred Indian servants and the command of the Army of the Northern Frontier. While the army had only thirty men and no uniforms, supplies or guns, it was still the largest and best army in the area—until Frémont's army arrived.

Frémont's instructions were to seize California as soon as the United States and Mexico declared war. Spurred on by determined American settlers, Frémont entered Sonoma on June 25. On July 5, a meeting of settlers chose him to direct the affairs of the "Republic of California."

Vallejo was ready. Several months earlier, he told some skeptical Mexican officials in Monterey, "Prepare for the glorious change that awaits our country. Why should we shrink from incorporating ourselves with the happiest and freest nation of the world?" Vallejo readily surrendered the Army of the Northern Frontier and prepared to become an American. At noon, on July 9th, the American flag was raised over the plaza of Yerba Buena.

In only two years, the town, renamed San Francisco, boasted two hotels, twelve stores, a billiard hall, a bowling alley and two newspapers. John Marsh and Vallejo made a fortune selling beef to the growing city. John C. Frémont was less fortunate.

When the United States Army, under General Stephen Kearny, arrived in California two weeks after Frémont's triumph, Frémont refused to relinquish his authority. He insisted that Yerba Buena chose him and he was thus entitled to run it. General Kearny pointed out that he had orders to establish a new government, but Frémont refused to yield. When Kearny returned East, Frémont followed, a prisoner bound for court-martial.

Although President Polk remitted the sentence, Frémont still felt the disgrace. Now, in 1849, after the discovery of gold, Frémont resigned from the Army and set out on an expedition to find a railroad route across the mountains. His wife, Jessie, followed by ship.

Frémont set off on this trip without his regular guides, Kit Carson and Broken-Hand Fitzpatrick. In their place, he took Old Bill Williams of Pueblo, Colorado. Old Bill had a beaded buckskin jacket, clear gray eyes, a salty vocabulary, but no sense of direction. Within two weeks, Frémont's men, carrying seventy-pound packs across fifteen-foot snowdrifts in temperatures below zero, became completely lost in the San Juan Mountains. When a rescue party from Taos finally found them, Old Bill was unconscious and eleven of Frémont's men were dead. A badly frostbitten Frémont was helped to Taos where he left for California to meet Jessie.

Ten days after the *Panama* docked, Frémont walked

16

into Jessie's room and without a word hugged her. Because he had had enough of mountains and Jessie wanted him to be with Lily, they bought a prefabricated wooden house. The house, imported from China, had to be assembled like a puzzle. Together they built their home on a tiny lot in the southern part of the city. Next, they hired a Mexican cook and nailed together a table from loose shingles so they could entertain.

Meanwhile, Dr. Gwin, portmanteau in hand, carefully picked his way through the streets, trying to avoid getting dust and mud on his suit. He was looking for the house of a merchant whose importance was sufficient to open his campaign for the United States Senate.

When Sam Ward and Hall McAllister got off the *Panama,* they were ravenously hungry. They asked directions to a restaurant and someone pointed up Telegraph Hill. They trudged through crowds of miners, stalled wagons, piles of lumber and teamsters wrestling with mules until they found a large number of men sitting around upended barrels under a large canvas awning. They sat at an empty barrel. A man in an apron told them that the menu was pork and beans. After a considerable time, the man brought them two tin plates of pork and beans which Ward and McAllister devoured in seconds. They caught the attention of the man with the apron again and asked how much they owed him. "Eight dollars," the man said. McAllister and Ward looked at each other. Moments later they almost ran down the hill to get their crates of food and supplies from the ship.

Soon Ward and McAllister pitched a tent in a vacant lot and pried open their crates of supplies. Within an hour, their tent was jammed with customers.

As a joke, McAllister hung his father's shingle reading,

"M. Hall McAllister, Attorney-at-Law." A group of sailors, taking the sign at face value, begged McAllister to represent them in a dispute over pay with their captain. McAllister, who had not practiced law, was reluctant, but Ward urged him on. When the sailors brought their New York attorney before the captain, he surrendered. McAllister won his first case.

In the following weeks, Ward bought an abandoned ship, which he converted and made the city's first department store. McAllister, bolstered by his first victory, rented a room and hung out his own shingle.

Before long Ward and McAllister became regular guests at the Frémonts' house, regaling Jessie with tales of adventure, while Frémont and Dr. Gwin talked politics in the back room. For Ward and McAllister, talk was the mainstay of social success. "Went to dance last night," Ward wrote in his diary. "Didn't have much fun. The girls spoke only Spanish." If the fandango halls failed, there was gambling. Ward soon lost heavily in a faro game. For Jessie, with only sixteen women in the city considered respectable enough to be introduced to her, the social possibilities were limited.

Culture arrived in San Francisco on June 22, 1849, with Stephen Massett. All over the city posters announced that, for three dollars, one would be permitted to hear and gaze upon the composer of "When the Moon on the Lake Is Beaming."

On that day, chairs and a piano were carried across the plaza to the old police court, transforming it into a concert hall. A sign was hung reserving the first row for ladies. At eight o'clock, four ladies occupied the front chairs of the sold-out concert hall. Massett, in splendid evening dress, stepped through the door, bowed deeply and accepted the cheers of his audience.

With a fine quaver in his voice, he began with his own composition, "When the Moon on the Lake Is Beaming," causing the four ladies in the front row to blush. There was rapturous applause when he finished. Massett continued with lines from Richard III, and did impressions of a Frenchman and a Yankee, an old woman and a German girl, each in a different voice. The audience was enthralled.

At his recital of a dramatic poem entitled "The Loss of the Steamship President," the audience was visibly shaken when the ship broke in a thousand pieces, hurling its passengers to the Pacific. To lighten the mood, he sang "I'm Sitting on the Stile, Mary," and did an impression of a New York razor strop man.

The finale, a New England town debate using seven different voices, brought the house down. The audience leaped to its feet; their clapping and cheers could be heard a block away.

2. THE CHIVALRY AND THE SHOVELRY

Such a gathering of beauty and fashion was never before seen in San Francisco. However, there were negative comments. It was felt that such relics of the rural dancing academy as the schottische and polka had not been in vogue since Noah's first reception on the Ark and had long since, in Boston, New York and Washington ceded to the waltz, the lancers, galop and quadrille. It was a disgrace for San Francisco to have such antiquated steps.

> Grand Centennial Ball, February 22, 1876, from Julia Altrocchi's *The Spectacular San Franciscans,* 1949.

In anticipation of California's admission to the union, two men were selected to represent the state by the legislature in San Jose. John C. Frémont, "The Pathfinder," as he was known, and Dr. William McKendree Gwin, the distinguished former congressman and one-time personal secretary of Andrew Jackson, became the state's first senators in September, 1850.

Gwin and Frémont, accompanied by Sam Ward carrying a suitcase of gold nuggets, recounted the changes that had taken place since the 1849 Christmas fire that left San Francisco a smoldering ruin. Now, Ward was going to New York to show his gold to the relatives who had scoffed at his fortunes. Gwin and Frémont were on their way to Washington. Cheered by a crowd of well-wishers, these first ambassadors of the golden kingdom sailed from the Bay on January 1, 1850.

The old residents sat in Delmonico's recently built saloon on Montgomery Street. Cattle still grazed there (the street was unpaved), but now they were the exception rather than the rule. The general preoccupation of these old-timers was the fact that they had been the first and were entitled to more recognition than was commonly accorded them.

In August 1850 opportunity in the shape of the steamer *California* paddled into the Bay, her enormous American flag at half-mast and her masts draped in black crepe. As she neared the dock, her crew shouted that President Zachary Taylor was dead.

Soon church bells—the number of churches nearly matched the number of saloons in San Francisco—were tolling all over town. In that volatile city, a funeral observance was as grand a social event as the Fourth of July or a hanging. Firemen began unpacking their best red shirts and sashes, the California Guard started polishing their bayonets and the brass buttons of their uniforms and the Masons began marching in step; there was going to be a parade.

At Delmonico's, James Wadsworth, who had come to San Francisco in 1847, suggested the original settlers march together in the parade. A noisy argument ensued. Was an original settler someone who had come two years earlier or three years earlier? To eliminate Johnny-come-latelies, they settled on three years. William Davis Merry Howard (a merchant who had come to San Francisco in the 1830s as a cabin boy) and his partner Talbot Green offered their warehouse as a meeting place. Sam Brannan, who led two hundred Mormons in 1846, offered to print a notice in his paper, the *Star*.

On the morning of the parade, the entire city was

22

festooned with black crepe, American flags and portraits that were supposed to resemble Zachary Taylor. The citizenry stood, hats respectfully in hand, while cornets tooted, drums thumped, and bands, firemen, soldiers, Masons and horse-drawn floats of Taylor's life passed by. A banner proclaiming "The Pioneers of California" was followed by a solemn Sam Brannan on horseback leading a procession of fifty men. This was the beginning of organized society in San Francisco, the first link of the Golden Circle.

From the very day it was founded, the Society of California Pioneers had the distinction of being completely useless. Its members drank toasts to compliment themselves on their superior wisdom in arriving in California before January 1, 1848, instead of after. On the common ground that they had been there longer than anyone else, they became the quintessence of society.

After much deliberation, they designed for themselves a gold-fringed, silk banner showing a pioneer stepping ashore by the Golden Gate. More argument established a twenty-five man board to govern the fifty-eight-member society. William D. M. Howard was elected president, Talbot Green treasurer, and Mariano Vallejo was among the three vice-presidents.

When California was admitted to the Union they unfurled their new banner for the parade and joined in the cannon salutes, celebrations and general uproar that followed. This success inspired them for the New Year. The Grand Ball they sponsored demolished the largest hall in town, put most of the members in bed for a week and bankrupted the society's treasury. Treasurer Green, to the general acclaim of the membership, reached into his own pocket to pay the seven-hundred-dollar debt.

Green was still basking in this affection when a visitor from Philadelphia saw him and announced that he was not Green, but a bank embezzler named Paul Geddes.

The Pioneers reacted with indignation. They had never heard such a damnable slander. They gathered at the Eagle Saloon to drink toasts and exchange testaments to their treasurer. "May the best among us be as worthy as we believe him to be," one toasted. Then Green himself rose to denounce the slanderer and announce he would sail to Philadelphia that night to win complete vindication. The Pioneers cheered and escorted him to the dock where he boarded the *Panama*. Because he was Paul Geddes, the bank embezzler from Philadelphia, he was arrested and put in prison when his ship docked.

Hearing the news, the Pioneers shrugged and elected a new treasurer, William Tecumseh Sherman, a humorless banker and former army officer. But they were loyal enough to Green to insist the city name a street after him and it did.

Mariano Vallejo worked hard at being a good American. He observed that Americans picked places in the middle of nowhere, gave them extravagant names and sold the land in parcels to people who expected new cities to develop.

He had a fair amount of land, the seventy-thousand-acre Rancho Petaluma. The spot he picked north of San Francisco seemed the place for a new metropolis. He bought the land and named it Benicia, after his wife Francisca Benicia Carillo, and sat back to await development.

He waited a long time. For one year in 1853, Benicia was the capital of California, but then the legislature transferred to Sacramento. Oakland, San Mateo, Sacramento and San Jose became cities, but not Benicia.

In New York, Sam Ward enjoyed a few glorious weeks of revenge. One night he pelted his ex-wife Medora's window with gold nuggets. Then he tried to open a branch of his store in New York but found that the flair and extravagance that made him a success in San Francisco were frowned upon in sedate Manhattan. Chastened, he returned to San Francisco with his brother-in-law, Adolph Mailliard. Mailliard promptly bought a ranch north of San Francisco and then returned to his villa in Bordentown, New Jersey to await the birth of his first child.

John Frémont was less than a success as a United States senator. The "Pathfinder of the Sierras" found the labyrinthine cloakrooms of the Senate more impenetrable than the West. Still suffering from the effects of his last experience in the mountains, he attended few sessions. Frémont left the Senate in frustration in 1851. Thanks to his ownership of a gold mine in California, he was a millionaire. At Jessie's urging, they went to Paris. Their second daughter was born there in 1853, but died in infancy. A third child, Francis, was born in 1854.

Senator Gwin fared much better. His mellifluous voice, southern manners and elegant opinions on everything from political philosophy to astronomy won him a place in every salon in Washington, including the White House. Characteristically, Gwin lectured his enthralled listeners on the glorious future of the western coast, the splendor of San Francisco Bay and the awesome majesty of redwood trees; when the conversation turned to politics, as it invariably did, Gwin had the statesman's ability to bluntly and unequivocally tell his listeners what they already believed.

While Senator Gwin talked, his wife, Mary Bell smiled and studied the guests, sorting them into those she wanted to know and should flatter, those she could cheerfully condescend to and those she could dismiss with a quick smile and a handshake. The daughter of a Virginia tavern keeper, she had learned the social skills the hard way. She knew whom to visit and whom to allow oneself to be visited by; whom to honor and whom to shun; how to judge a person's rank in moments; and how to speak with a single gesture and say absolutely nothing in an afternoon. Having learned the basic skills, she applied herself to the more sweeping matters of strategy. With the graciousness and self-assurance of a woman who believed she was as good as anyone and better than most, Mary Bell kept her eyes open for advancement, while protecting her flanks and rear from social climbers and parvenues.

Being the wife of a United States senator was exactly what she wanted. She worked hard for Gwin and made a point of being devoted to San Francisco. She even changed her birthday to the day the *Panama* brought her husband to California. Staying in hotels and having to rub shoulders with gamblers, stock speculators and men with New York accents was the one thing she did not appreciate.

These opinions were shared by many other southerners in San Francisco who proudly called themselves the "Chivalry." The merchants and men who had made their fortunes in the mines were dismissed as the "Shovelry." Beside Mrs. Gwin, the Chivalry's leaders were the twin sisters Mrs. Peter Donahue and Mrs. Eleanor Martin, Mrs. John McMullin, the Milton Lathams, the Thomas Selbys and Mrs. Abby Eastman Meagher Parrott who, although born in Maine, was entitled to a place in the Chivalry because her husband, John Parrott, was a

Virginian and a former consul to Mazatlan. Together, the Chivalry decided to establish a place to hold court.

Rincon Hill, just south of the center of the city, was selected as the first site. It boasted a pleasant view of the Bay, was just far enough from downtown to be out of earshot of the hammering and crashing of the city, yet it was a short carriage ride to the men's offices. It was also reasonably free of the fog that drifted across much of the city every summer afternoon.

A large square on the north side of the hill was cleared of sheep and debris and an iron fence was built around it. Outside the fence, a street was laid out like a miniature racetrack. A small windmill was erected inside the fence to irrigate the cultivated lawn. On one side of the little park, a row of square brick houses was constructed. Each one was decorated with tinted windows and a wrought-iron balcony. The contractor claimed it was an exact replica of Berkeley Square in London.

The Chivalry moved from their hotels to the new neighborhood, christened "South Park." Among them was Hall McAllister. Only Mrs. Abby Eastman Meagher Parrott was reluctant to move. Her husband owned the New Almaden Quicksilver mine, and possessed probably the largest fortune in the city. She was proud to be numbered among the Chivalry but felt she was more than the Chivalry. She was especially hesitant to be a common tenant in a row of houses. After considerable thought, the problem was solved; Mrs. Parrott constructed a house on Rincon Hill, close to, but just above South Park. Her new house looked exactly like a bank vault with a Greek portico.

At Christmas, oyster suppers and eggnog soirees were the fashion among the Chivalry. When the New Year approached, one of the women told of a Dutch custom in old New York, whereby bachelors made formal calls on the first day of the year and were received by the young ladies with cakes and small glasses of wine. This seemed a charming idea, so invitations were sent and houses were decorated on New Year's Eve.

In the morning, the bachelors began arriving. Their arrivals were irregular. Often they didn't seem quite certain where they were, since most of them had been up all night drinking a unique San Francisco beverage called a "Brandy Smash." The young hostesses were prepared for that, but they had forgotten that the rains in December turned the streets of San Francisco into waterways. Montgomery Street was like the Mississippi River; South Park was like Lake Erie. Cheerfully the bachelors tramped through the entry halls of the houses on Rincon Hill, coated with mud up to their knees. The hostesses smiled bravely as their mothers' expensive Brussels carpets took the appearance of mule trails. Even this, however, could be turned to social advantage. For weeks afterward, visible proof of a young lady's popularity was imprinted in her carpet.

In the evenings there were long suppers. One, at the home of Isaac Friedlander, began at six-thirty with oysters on the half shell and moved at a leisurely pace through soup, prawn salad, baked sole, beef, roast turkey, asparagus, quail, terrapin, meringue, fruit with cream and brandy, cakes, candied fruits, oranges, apples, pears and grapes, accompanied by sherry, sauterne, burgundy, port, liqueurs and champagne. When the women finally rose and moved to the drawing room and the men pushed back their chairs and lit up cigars, it was well after midnight.

The women talked about novels, Paris couture and about the new families in town. There was, for instance, a new doctor, an army surgeon named Dr. Charles McPhail Hitchcock and his wife, the former Martha Hunter of North Carolina. They had a seven-year-old daughter named Eliza Whychie Hitchcock. Her father, who thought she was as lovely as a flower, called her Lillie. Lillie had been playing in a half-finished building when one of the city's regular fires had swept through it. She had been rescued by a fireman from the volunteer company named Knickerbocker Number Five. Her grateful father gave Knickerbocker Number Five a thousand dollars, for a new fire engine, and a barrel of brandy. It was said that Lillie now got very excited when a fire engine passed by. The women laughed; she would soon get over that. In the next room, the men's gossip was called politics.

John C. Frémont was back from Paris. He had proved himself a genius as an explorer, but less than competent as a politician. Whether through character or circumstance, Frémont promptly went back into politics. The brand-new Republican Party selected him as their first presidential candidate in 1856. Frémont chose the celebrated William L. Dayton, a former United States senator from New Jersey, over an ambitious but inexperienced Illinois congressman named Lincoln, as his vicepresidential candidate. Even Dayton's prestige and a catchy slogan: "Free Soil, Free Land, Free Men and Frémont," were not enough to win. The novice Frémont was soundly beaten by the veteran politician James Buchanan. After the election, Frémont, Jessie and the children returned to San Francisco. He bought a large house on a rocky point jutting into the Bay far from the center of the city. Disenchanted by politics, city life and people, Frémont accepted the leadership of an expedition looking for transcontinental railway routes.

Jessie added a glass-walled veranda to the house to enhance the view of the Bay. She entertained not only the Chivalry, but the merchants of the city and other writers and artists. Bret Harte and Herman Melville sat at her table, as did Richard Henry Dana, the author of *Two Years Before the Mast.* After a visit he wrote admiringly that she was "a heroine equal to either fortune, the salons of Paris and the drawing rooms of New York and Washington, or the roughest life of the remote and wild regions of Mariposa." The Chivalry was willing to grant that she was a pleasing hostess, even though she was a northerner.

Whether one was a northerner or a southerner suddenly became important. There was a feeling in the air that things were somehow out of control, that the country was sliding toward something ominous. The newspapers carried accounts of hostile debates in Washington, even of a senator being caned on the floor of the Senate. Senator Gwin's words to the Senate, "I say that a dissolution of the Union is not impossible, that it is not impracticable," were read in San Francisco. Sides were being taken.

Mary Bell Gwin wanted to ignore it. She gave a spectacular costume ball in her Washington mansion. Mr. and Mrs. Jefferson Davis were there, as were Mr. and Mrs. Stephen Douglas. Mary Bell Gwin, costumed as the wife of Louis XIV, swept into the ballroom on the arm of President Buchanan himself. But the next morning, out of costume, the debate continued—no less bitter than before. In fact, the two senators from California were hardly speaking to one another.

Frémont's place in the Senate had been taken by a genial Irishman with curly black hair named David Broderick. Broderick's father was one of the stonemasons who built the United States Capitol building. The young Broderick came to San Francisco in 1849 to join the gold rush. He found his fortune, not in the mountains, but right in San Francisco. Because the miners complained about having to carry awkward sacks of gold dust, he began his own mint, coining five-dollar gold pieces. Since the coins contained only four dollars worth of gold, he was soon wealthy.

His fortune secure, he turned to politics. He was an awkward speaker, but he was outgoing and traveled tirelessly to all the mining camps where he ate, drank and spoke with the miners about workingmen's issues. Their votes elected him to the Senate. He took a seat in the chamber his father helped build.

The Chivalry considered Broderick a perfect example of Shovelry; his awkward speech amused them. He was not invited to Mary Bell Gwin's costume ball. In San Francisco, David Terry, a judge of the state supreme court, a Texan and a member of the Chivalry, spoke disdainfully to a local Democratic gathering. "Broderick's professed following of Douglas meant not Stephen Douglas the statesman, but Frederick Douglass the mulatto."

Broderick, reading the remark in the newspaper as he breakfasted in the dining room of the International Hotel, told a friend that he no longer considered Terry an honest man. One of Terry's friends at a nearby table

heard the remark, leaped up, strode over to Broderick
and, on behalf of Terry, demanded he withdraw the
remark or be challenged to a duel. Broderick refused.

To the Chivalry, the charge was serious; they had the
custom of dueling over "affairs of honor." The editor of
one newspaper was forced to post a sign in his office
reading, "Subscriptions received from 9 to 4: challenges
from 11 to 12 only."

Soon, all San Francisco knew what Terry and Broderick had said. Terry sent a challenge to Broderick.
Broderick refused it. Terry sent another challenge, then
another, implying that Broderick was a coward if he did
not accept. Broderick accepted.

The duel was set at dawn on September 13, 1859, near
Lake Merced. Terry and his seconds were ready when
Broderick and his seconds arrived in a carriage. Some
sixty shivering spectators waited nearby.

The seconds discussed the rules in quiet voices. Terry
was awarded the choice of weapons. His second produced
a case containing two Lafoucheux dueling pistols, notorious for firing at the slightest touch. Terry and Broderick
each took a pistol and stepped back. As the spectators
watched in silence, the two men stepped back until they
were ten paces apart. When the second asked, "Gentlemen, are you ready?" both men raised their pistols. The
second began to count.

At the count of one, Broderick's pistol went off with a
sharp crack; the bullet fired into the ground. The trigger
had not been touched. With the empty pistol in his hand,
Broderick stood helplessly as the second continued
counting.

At the count of three, Terry took careful aim at
Broderick. The pistol cracked; its bullet went through

the center of Broderick's chest. Broderick dropped to his knees and fell face forward onto the sand. Three days later, he died.

The workingmen, miners and small merchants may not have understood the issues being debated in Washington, but they knew Broderick. On the day of his funeral nearly every business closed and most of the buildings in San Francisco were draped in black crepe. At his funeral service in the plaza, thirty thousand San Franciscans paid tribute. For the first time, the Shovelry were united.

On Rincon Hill, in South Park, the blinds were drawn and the residents remained secluded. The Civil War had come to San Francisco. Terry's single shot had not only killed Broderick, it mortally wounded the Chivalry.

Business went on, oblivious of society or politics. A twenty-year-old Bavarian Jew named Levi Strauss cut up the canvas tents he had brought from the east to sell to the miners. Miners had complained to him that chunks of ore tore right through the pockets of their cotton trousers, so he determined to make trousers from canvas, securely fastening the pockets with rivets.

James Folger, who worked as a carpenter on a coffee mill when he arrived, became intrigued with the coffee business. After mining a small quantity of gold, he bought a store in a mining town and earned enough to return to San Francisco, where he opened his own coffee business. He met the ships carrying sacks of coffee beans from South America and sorted them shoulder to shoulder with other local coffee merchants. Among these were the Hills brothers, Austin and Reuben, and Max Joseph Brandenstein, whose sacks of coffee beans bore his initials, M.J.B.

Heinrich Alfred Kreiser arrived from Germany in 1850 with six dollars. Because he learned butchering in New York, he was soon able to get a job in a San Francisco meat shop. The frugal Kreiser saved enough money for his own shop and then his own ranch. Before long, he owned over a million head of cattle. Changing his name to Henry Miller, the proud immigrant bought a house in South Park and moved in next to the Chivalry.

In the new brick banks and exchanges downtown, the efforts of Andrew Pope, who founded a lumber and shipping firm, Aaron Fleishacker, a one-time storekeeper in the Sierra mining camps, and Louis Sloss, who traded furs from Alaska, were turning the city into a major West Coast commercial center.

Claus Spreckels, a German immigrant, who worked in a grocery store, noticed that all the sugar he sold had been grown in Hawaii, shipped to the East Coast to be refined, and then shipped back to San Francisco. He felt there was money in a cheaper way.

He took a ship to Honolulu where his foresight was assisted by good luck; he won a large part of the island of Maui in a poker game with King Kalakua. There he built a sugar refinery and when he learned the tricks of the business, sold it, moved back to San Francisco and built another sugar mill.

Not only coffee merchants haunted the docks. Two Sacramento shopkeepers often stood with them. The lean, nonsmoking, nondrinking vegetarian Mark Hopkins bought all the blankets he could get, hauled them to a warehouse in Sacramento and stashed them away until winter. Then the price skyrocketed. The two-hundred-fifty-pound Charles Crocker, who charged around the dock like a bull, shouting at the men on ships, and swearing at the longshoremen, dwarfed Mark Hopkins. He and his brother had come from Indiana and spent two years searching for gold. Finally, they decided to open a store. The store became their gold mine. It succeeded so well that they opened a Sacramento branch, which Charles ran.

Hopkins' partner, Collis Huntington, had, at fourteen, saved up a hundred dollars; then he began selling butter and peddling jewelry. When he came to California, he carried a shipload of goods with which he stocked and opened a store in Sacramento. Hopkins did the accounting and kept the stock in order; Huntington did the moving and bought the merchandise. In a tiny rowboat in the middle of the Bay, Huntington peered at arriving ships through binoculars. When the ship he was watching got close Huntington would row alongside, board, pull out a sack of gold dust he had tied around his waist and begin bargaining with the astonished captain. Before the other merchants even knew the ship arrived, Huntington would have bought its entire cargo.

The Chivalry disdained these men. But these Shovelry would before long push the Chivalry aside to take their place in the Golden Circle of San Francisco society.

3. CASTLES AND KINGS

With great celebration the first transcontinental telegraph line between San Francisco and Washington was opened on November 6, 1862. San Francisco was no longer a distant outpost, but a corner of the Union. After the first congratulatory messages came through, the wire was full of war bulletins.

The Pony Express brought news of the election of Lincoln, the secession of South Carolina and the firing on Fort Sumter two years before. In South Park, the Chivalry celebrated. John C. Frémont and William Tecumseh Sherman promptly packed their trunks and sailed east to join the Union Army. Jessie Frémont was told the army needed the point of land on which her house stood, so she, too, packed and left. A few weeks later the glass veranda was pulled down, and brick walls laid in its place. Cannon aimed out at the Bay.

David Terry sailed for the South to join the Confederate Army. Senator Gwin, whose son Willie was already in the Confederate Army, was arrested on shipboard by Union officers who accused him of trying to enlist some of their men in the Confederate cause; he was put in a prison near the Capitol, until President Lincoln learned he was there and ordered him freed. He and Mary Bell gathered their family and sailed for Paris to await the end of the war.

Lillie Hitchcock, an outspoken rebel sympathizer, now eighteen, had been sent to Paris. Her proud mother wanted her to be a southern belle; she already looked the part and with half the bachelors in San Francisco in love with her, she had been engaged fifteen times. Her mother saw the dark-haired girl with merry brown eyes presiding graciously in a South Park mansion, playing the piano, reading Sir Walter Scott novels and taking fifteen minutes to say what a northerner would say in five. That was what gentility was all about. But Lillie, her mother admitted with some embarrassment, still chased fire engines. She went, in fact, to every fire. She had even run from a wedding rehearsal in her bridesmaid's gown to chase a fire engine up Telegraph Hill. Mrs. Hitchcock's friends consoled her; this was a phase that would pass. Mrs. Hitchcock expected much from the serene grandeur of Paris.

She received reports of her daughter's progress eagerly. Lillie was received at Court, Lillie engaged in conversation with the Empress Eugenie, Lillie was translating Confederate war dispatches for the Emperor Napoleon III, and, she had the most charming habit of chasing fire engines.

While most of San Francisco talked about the war, four shopkeepers were discussing a railroad. Charles

Crocker, Mark Hopkins, Collis Huntington and a whole-sale grocer named Leland Stanford met in 1856, in Sacramento at a Republican gathering. Supporters of John C. Frémont for president, they now turned their interest to a transcontinental railroad.

This long-cherished dream of Californians was the brainchild of a young engineer named Theodore Judah. Judah had charts, maps, tables, surveyor's reports and pages of testimony saying a railroad could come through the mountains. With the right amount of money, California's isolation could be ended. To prove his point, in the 1850s he actually built the twenty-one-mile Sacramento Valley Railroad, inspiring Stephen Massett, the com-poser of "When the Moon on the Lake Is Beaming," to write still another song, "Clear the Way," or "The Song of the Wagon-Road."

Crocker, Huntington, Stanford and Hopkins were con-vinced less by the romance of forcing a railroad through the mountains than by the amount of money the govern-ment would pay them to try. They required only ten percent of the value of the stock (less than $7000); the government would loan them $16,000 to $32,000 for each mile of line, plus millions of acres of land along the way.

Mark Hopkins, their treasurer, calculated the fortune they would make. The only people who would make more money than they, the owners of the railroad, would be the contractors they hired to build the railroad.

Soon afterward the directors of the Central Pacific Railroad, Leland Stanford, Collis Huntington, Mark Hopkins and Charles Crocker, announced they had hired a construction company to build their railroad. The directors of the new construction company were Crocker, Hopkins, Huntington and Stanford. Theodore Judah, who expected to be chief engineer of the railroad, was informed that his services were no longer required. Furious, Judah went to New York by ship to fight the decision. When crossing the isthmus of Panama, he caught yellow fever and died.

On January 8, 1863, accompanied by an enthusiastic band, Stanford, the president of the Central Pacific Railroad, dug the first shovelful of earth from the bank of the Sacramento River and dropped it into a flag-draped wagon. The railroad was under construction.

Stanford, tall, bearded, and immensely dignified, was not only the president of the railroad, but also the governor of California. As the first Republican governor, his job was to give prestige to the enterprise. His public pronouncements were so earnest, so lengthy, so verbose and so boring that it was impossible to believe that he, no less the railroad, were anything but solid and honest.

Huntington dealt with Congress and bought materials for the railroad. When Congress offered $32,000 a mile to lay track in the foothills and $16,000 a mile to lay track on the flatlands, Huntington accepted. When he had the new map of California drawn, he moved the Sierra Nevada Mountains twenty-five miles west of their actual location. By coincidence, this spot was right where the Central Pacific began.

Uncle Mark Hopkins, as Hopkins was called, was a self-appointed money-saver. Each day he walked through the railroad offices peering into the wastebaskets for usable scraps of paper. When he toured the tracks, he habitually picked up old bolts and rusty bits of metal, put them in his pocket and hoped they might become useful.

The big red-bearded Charles Crocker actually built the railroad. In his zealousness, he joyously wasted every penny that Hopkins saved. He stood with workers in the rain, sweated with them in the sun, swore at them and drove the railroad up the side of the mountains. When the white workers deserted to the silver fields, he replaced them with sixteen thousand Chinese, saying, "They built the great wall of China, didn't they?" A huge figure on horseback, Crocker paid the workers himself. Carrying gold coins in one saddlebag and silver in the other, he rode among the thousands of blue-bloused Chinese like a Manchu emperor. Week after week he lived in his private railroad car, traveling between the railhead and the supply camps in the rear, watching the men dig by day and poring over charts and survey reports in his swaying railway car at night.

While men hauled, blasted and chipped away at the rock, cleared the snow and were swept into the canyons by avalanches or blown to bits by dynamite, Crocker raged and exhorted behind them. When they reached the granite spine of the mountains, the pig-tailed Chinese worked twelve-hour shifts around the clock drilling through the rock. Under such conditions they moved only eight inches a day, but finally they broke through. Crocker was alongside them, as they began driving down the other side.

Since the profits were double the cost of laying track, the race between the Union Pacific in the East and the Central Pacific in the West became even more furious. Crocker laid track through the eastern foothills and began unrolling track in the Nevada desert in 120-degree heat at the rate of a mile of track a day. He supervised all on horseback, his head covered like a bedouin sheik. In New York, Huntington commanded a fleet of ships that hauled track and locomotives from the East Coast to San Francisco, where they were put on trains to

Crocker's camp in the Nevada desert. Hopkins kept track of the expenses and saw that they were passed on to Washington. Meantime, Stanford, dignified as always, traveled ahead of the railroad, solemnly shaking hands with local dignitaries, giving speeches and making promises.

On May 10, 1869, six years after they began, the two railroads met at Promontory, Utah. Five hundred people stood along the tracks as the flag-draped locomotives, one facing east, the other west, slowly approached each other, stopping a few feet apart.

A polished California laurel tie was laid in place in the track; the point of a golden spike was fitted into it. A wire ran from the spike to a telegraph transmitter nearby. Another wire was attached to the silver hammer which was handed to Leland Stanford. When Stanford hit the spike, it would work as a rude telegraph key and the click would be heard throughout the United States. Meanwhile, a telegrapher was busy tapping out an account of the ceremonies. After delivering a very long "short" address, Stanford stepped to the undriven spike. The crowd hushed. Stanford raised the hammer, swung it through the air in a whistling arc, and missed the spike. The telegrapher tactfully clicked his key once.

In San Francisco, fire bells, church bells and cannon firing could be heard even in the stately houses on South Park and Rincon Hill. The city was linked to the rest of the nation. Over that link would soon come the wealth that would build the greatest fortunes in the West.

The Civil War ended in 1865, but for the Chivalry it lasted another ten years. They fought to keep the social position accorded them by birth and to keep the nouveau riche from their circle. Thanks to the railroad, this was a losing battle. Wealth poured into San Francisco, mansions rose all over town. The pleasant sanctuary of South Park was being surrounded by warehouses and factories. Soon the din of machinery and railroad whistles would drown the piano playing.

A six-foot-tall, athletic-looking man named William Ralston had been a clerk on a Mississippi steamboat before he entered the bullion business and came to San Francisco. He invested in the Central Pacific Railroad, in vineyards, in real estate, in a woolen mill, a clock factory and a dozen other enterprises. When he became cashier of his own bank, the Bank of California, he had a respectable fortune. Now he was to be one of the first of a unique San Francisco breed—the overnight multimillionaire.

This deluge of wealth came from the silver that underlay Virginia City, Nevada. Ralston owned stock in some of the silver mines there, but even he was surprised by the incredibly rich veins his miners found. The Comstock Lode, as this bonanza was called, turned out to be one of the richest finds in the history of mining. Germany was forced to go off the silver standard, residents of Virginia City fitted their horses with silver horseshoes, and William Ralston became one of the richest men in San Francisco.

Before the bonanza Ralston had been a man of modestly expensive tastes. Now he learned to spend with the prodigality of the Pharoah Rameses. He rebuilt the Bank of California, of which he was president, in the style of a Roman temple only slightly less ornate than St. Peter's Basilica. In a city of two hundred thousand people, he began what would become the largest and most expensive hotel in the world. Twenty miles south of San

Francisco, in Belmont, he constructed the most extraordinary country mansion in California.

Whenever a foreign dignitary or industrial baron from the East came to San Francisco, Ralston would take them by coach to Belmont. He would explain that he had bought the house from an exiled Italian nobleman named Count Cipriani, adding a few innovations of his own. The first of these was shown to the startled visitor as the carriage approached the house; as the carriage clattered across a small bridge, its weight tripped a system of levers and counterweights that flung open the gates of the courtyard.

Once inside the front door, Ralston led his guest through a spacious entrance hall, lighted by skylights, through etched-glass doorways to his private oval ballroom. The balustrades of the balconies and stairways in the ballroom and even the doorknobs were all silver.

Ralston was not the only overnight millionaire. William O'Brien and James Flood came to San Francisco in 1849, O'Brien from Dublin, Flood from New York. They met in the mining camp of Poor Man's Gulch and both decided to open shops in San Francisco. O'Brien opened a livery and carriage store and Flood started a marine supply shop, but both were wiped out by fire in 1855. They combined what little they had left, swallowed their pride and opened a bar in the financial district called the Auction Lunch.

O'Brien, dressed in a high silk hat, stood outside and appealed to passerbys to come inside, where Flood, also dressed in a silk hat and business suit, stood behind the counter slicing corned beef and pouring drinks. Since the San Francisco Stock Exchange was only a few doors away, the Auction Lunch was regularly crowded with brokers. Flood and O'Brien were sympathetic to their problems and listened carefully. Each night, after closing, they wrote down the names of the best stocks and the next morning, they added a little to their portfolio.

By 1868 they had made enough money in the stock market to sell the Auction Lunch and open their own brokerage house. Two mining engineers, John Mackay and James Fair, came to them from Virginia City. Mackay and Fair, unrolling diagrams of the Virginia City hillsides, argued that under extant mines there was even more silver; all they needed was the machinery to dig it out.

In any other respectable brokerage house (even in San Francisco), Mackay and Fair would have been shown the door. They had no solid evidence of silver, no engineers' reports, no letters of introduction, no established position. All they had was a hunch.

But Flood and O'Brien listened. When they finished listening, they wrote out a check for the mining machinery Mackay and Fair needed. Unlike New York or London brokers, they could gamble because they had nothing to lose. They had neither social position nor pretensions to uphold. If they had to, they could go back to running a saloon again without losing face.

As the magnitude of the Virginia City silver strike bonanza became obvious, San Francisco took on the appearance of an enormous gambling hall. Everyone was trying to buy stock, or knew what stock to buy, or had stock for sale. Worthless patches of Nevada desert were sold to eager speculators; each empty hole in a Virginia City hillside was advertised as the next King Solomon's mine. Everyone knew someone who knew someone else who had bought a mine with a few dollars one afternoon and had awakened the next morning, or sometimes just later that same afternoon, and found himself a multi-millionaire.

The fact that many of these stories were true made it exciting. Many empty holes in the hillsides did actually turn out to be virtually as rich as King Solomon's mines. Fortunes were made overnight, sometimes inadvertently. One speculator named E. S. Baldwin ordered his broker to sell his stock and then sailed to Hawaii on a business trip. When the broker gathered up the stock certificates, he found Baldwin had neglected to sign them so they couldn't be sold. Baldwin returned a few weeks later and found his stock was worth one hundred times the price at which he intended to sell it. From that day on, he was known as "Lucky" Baldwin.

Flood and O'Brien found that their gamble paid off. Mackay and Fair made a strike—a fifty-foot vein of silver that one engineer estimated was worth three hundred million dollars. Suddenly, the two bartenders and the two mining engineers were numbered among the richest men on earth.

This good fortune turned out to be a disaster for Ralston. The genial banker spent so lavishly on the Palace Hotel and on his house at Belmont that there was very little money left in the Bank of California. When O'Brien and Flood hit their bonanza, they took their money out of Ralston's bank to start their own. Following their star of glory, many San Franciscans decided to do the same thing. Unfortunately, there was too little money in the Bank of California to sustain this. Amid a tumultuous riot on Montgomery Street, Ralston ordered the doors of the bank shut. The next day, he went swimming in the Bay; a few hours later, his drowned body was carried ashore.

The sudden transformation from common person to multimillionaire had a curious effect on those San Franciscans fortunate enough to experience it. People who didn't know them looked on them with awe. Their most trivial word was listened to and repeated as though it had become the wisdom of the ages. At first, these world-wise businessmen must have thought it quite ridiculous, but after a while, they came to believe it themselves. After all, this was the age of Darwin; it was widely believed that God himself, through the process of natural selection, watched over every stock transaction and real estate deal, picking out those who would or would not get a fortune.

Some men, like O'Brien, Flood and Mackay carried their new wealth gracefully. They gave a great deal of money away and helped build a new San Francisco, without forgetting that they were just very fortunate mortals. Others, like James Fair, were not so modest.

Fair, a black-bearded, brooding Irishman, took great delight in making fools of other people. Habitually, he recommended mining stocks he knew to be worthless just for the pleasure of seeing people scramble to buy stock on the strength of his word. When the mines proved worthless and people lost their investments, Fair felt it justified his wisdom.

Even his wife was no exception to this policy. She asked him what stock to buy and he named a stock, warning her to tell no one. He knew she was a talkative person and would probably tell some of her friends, which she did. The stock, of course, was worthless; Mrs. Fair and her friends lost a small fortune. Fair paid his wife what she lost and told her that that should be a lesson to her.

This behavior destroyed Fair's popularity. His wife

divorced him, and his daughters did not even invite him to their weddings. Most of his days were spent in a tiny office, surrounded by models of mining machinery. The evenings he spent in his hotel room or in a tavern across the Bay in Sausalito, where he sat alone, hour after hour, drinking until he passed out.

One of William Ralston's business partners, a small, pale, reserved man named William Sharon, inherited Ralston's fortune, including his Palace Hotel and the house at Belmont. Unfortunately, he lacked Ralston's generosity. Sharon's chief desire was to be a United States senator. Unable to win election in California, Sharon established a legal residence in Virginia City, Nevada. By the simple expedient of giving each member of the Nevada Legislature a large number of shares in a silver mine he owned, Sharon was able to persuade them he was a statesman and friend of the people, deserving of a seat in the United States Senate. He was easily elected. After the election, Sharon sold the stock he owned in the silver mine, dropping the value of the Nevada legislators' stock from several hundred dollars to precisely nothing. The legislators, who could not tactfully admit they had accepted bribes, smoldered in silence.

San Francisco's new millionaires (particularly the wives of San Francisco's new millionaires) wanted to spend their enormous fortunes. This was more difficult than it seemed. How could one be extravagant in a town where the hotel clerks wore diamonds and the prostitutes wore Parisian gowns?

The most visible thing one could do was to own a large house, preferably a very large house situated on a high hill where everyone could see it. This realization set off an architectural orgy unrivaled in the West.

There was an unoccupied hill in the center of San Francisco—a bleak, windswept hill overlooking the financial district. Nameless until society chose it, it became known as Nob Hill, after the Moghul rulers, or Nabobs, of India, whose image society fancied.

It was unoccupied because it was too steep for any carriage to reach its top. The first, and for a long time only, resident of Nob Hill was an antisocial doctor named Hayne. He chose it in order to make it difficult for his patients to drop in at odd hours. When a local wire cable manufacturer named Andrew Hallidie invented a peculiar, crab-like coach that could scuttle to the top of the hill on one of his cables, it became a practical place to live.

In 1870, three years before Hallidie's cable car, three young businessmen contemplated the hill. One of them, Richard Tobin, thought it would be a suitable place for the founder of the Hibernia Bank to build his home. He hired an architect. Soon several dozen masons and carpenters were at work. When they finished, Richard Tobin showed his guests a three-story marble and mahogany grand staircase, a billiard room, library, chapel and a fifty-foot observation tower.

His friend, Lloyd Tevis, who came from Kentucky after the Civil War, built a second mansion near Tobin's home. When Tevis's guests toured his new house, they went one after another through eleven bedrooms, and then to the library, where, Tevis modestly admitted, he had shelved the largest collection of books on the West Coast.

James Haggin, Tevis's partner, brother-in-law and fellow Kentuckian, bought the entire city block bounded by Taylor, Mason, Washington and Jackson Streets. Soon another small army of carpenters, bricklayers, ironfitters and plumbers were swarming over the hill. Haggin's finished house was a four-story mansion standing in a terraced garden. Under the house in the cavernous stable, there was room for forty horses and eighteen carriages. Upstairs, there were fifty oak-paneled rooms, nine baths and an eighty-six-foot observation tower, which looked over the roof of Tevis's library and the top of Tobin's observation tower sixteen feet below.

That was only the beginning. Crocker, Hopkins, Huntington and Stanford were moving their headquarters from Sacramento to San Francisco. They, too, would need a place to live.

Mark Hopkins was in no hurry to build. He rented a small cottage on Sutter Street. The house was close enough to the railroad office for him to take a streetcar to work in the morning, and had a small backyard where he could putter in his vegetable garden when he came home.

Mary Hopkins was appalled by this arrangement. With one of the greatest fortunes in the United States, her husband was content to sell carrots and radishes from his garden to friends and neighbors. Not only did he sell them, but he sold them at a considerable profit. Mary served him her discontents until he agreed to build a mansion.

Mary Hopkins was a rather peculiar woman. Because Mark Hopkins was not exactly a *bon vivant,* and rarely traveled beyond the business perimeters of the Southern Pacific, she turned to herself for entertainment. A dedicated reader of novels, particularly the novels of Sir Walter Scott, she decided, as many did in those noisy, grubby days of the early industrial age, that the days of knighthood were the best of all possible times.

From his vegetable garden, Mark Hopkins saw the gothic castle, complete with battlements and spires, that his wife was building on Nob Hill. He never saw the completed house. While it was still under construction, he traveled to Arizona and had a heart attack. His private railway car was parked on a siding when he died.

Mary had the castle to herself. The three-story structure, its wood painted to resemble stone, was described by the architect as French. Beyond the turreted entrance and towering front door, a huge circular entrance hall led to a seventy-five-foot-long dining room, paneled in oak, that seated sixty. Beyond that was a ballroom, a music room and a library. Upstairs, off a gallery hung with medieval banners, were the bedrooms. Mary's room was supposed to be an exact replica of the bed chamber of the Duke of Milan. Its ebony-paneled walls were inlaid with ivory and semiprecious stones; its inner door was padded with velvet. When Mary Hopkins, surrounded by novels, lay back on her huge wood-posted bed, she looked up at a ceiling alive with angels and seraphim.

Leland Stanford, as president of the Southern Pacific and former governor of California, commanded enormous respect. If it was possible, he acted more dignified than before. When questioned, he paused and thoughtfully considered his reply, often for an entire minute, before answering. One interviewer considered this a very statesmanlike habit until, one morning, he asked the governor how he was feeling. Stanford looked thoughtful, pondered and almost a minute later answered, "Very well, thank you." He also had the habit of sitting so still when someone was talking to him that the other person became alarmed and questioned whether he was still alive.

The three other members of the Big Four thought none too highly of Stanford. Huntington said his contribution to the railroad was turning over the first shovelful of dirt and driving the last spike. Governor Stanford blithely ignored such criticism. He thrived on the glory due a railroad president; wherever his private car passed, all railroad employees were commanded to stand at attention and all locomotives were required to sound their whistles in salute.

He was a man of tremendous ceremony. When his first child, Leland Stanford, Jr., was born in 1868, Stanford invited his friends to a dinner party. A liveried waiter carried a covered silver platter to the table. "My friends," Stanford said solemnly, "I wish to introduce my son." The waiter uncovered the platter and there lay Leland Stanford, Jr., in a bed of flowers. The child was passed around the table for each of the guests to admire.

Stanford's mansion on Nob Hill was no surprise to anyone. It was larger and more majestic than any other building around it. Railroad engineers and masons laid a granite foundation on the side of the hill and built an enormous wooden box that resembled, Gertrude Atherton thought, "a packing crate painted white."

Inside the front door, a zodiac was laid in the marble floor. Seventy feet overhead, sunlight came through an amber glass skylight. There was, in addition, a Chinese room, furnished by the government of China; a mosaic-tiled Pompeian room; an art gallery, in the center of which was an artificial jungle complete with mechanical singing birds; a music room whose enormous music box could be heard throughout the house and finally, an East Indian reception room. Here, surrounded by mementos, honorary diplomas and ceremonial awards, Governor

Stanford, statuelike, expression frozen, received his guests.

Charles Crocker was, first and foremost, a builder. When the railroad was completed, he was given an office in the railroad's main building. Crocker fidgeted and paced in the office a few days, then left. He needed to be building something; it didn't seem to matter what, as long as it took him out of San Francisco. He was soon busy digging irrigation ditches in the San Joaquin Valley.

At a banquet, seated next to Governor Stanford, he was asked to speak. "All my life I've been a doer and not a talker," he said. "Some among the officials of this railroad's talents run to talking." Then he introduced Governor Stanford.

Mrs. Crocker, the former Mary Ann Deming of Mishawaka, Indiana, and the daughter of a mill owner, did not share her husband's joy in digging irrigation ditches. She insisted, as Mary Hopkins had, that they have a proper house on Nob Hill. Crocker finally agreed.

He bought a square block near the Stanford home, with the exception of a tiny corner which was owned by an undertaker named Yung. Knowing Crocker would need the land to finish his house, Yung refused Crocker's first offer. He sat back to await the next offer.

Yung underestimated the stubbornness of the man who had driven his railroad through the backbone of the Sierras. Instead of an offer, a small army of carpenters arrived and began hammering together a fantastic jigsaw puzzle of ornament, wooden balustrades, scrolls, bay windows, spires and gables that the architect, Arthur Brown, fondly described as "Early Renaissance." The result looked more like a cross between a Moorish palace and a railroad depot. Yung watched with dismay as this fantastic house rose on three sides of him. The final absurdity was a seventy-eight-foot observation tower. Then the carpenters set to work building a forty-foot wooden fence around the three sides of Yung's cottage, totally blocking its sunlight. The equally stubborn Yung remained in the house. Eventually, Yung sold his house to another man who sold it to Crocker.

But Crocker's wife wasn't finished. Now that she had a house, she was determined to furnish it in suitable style. At the time, this meant antiques and paintings from Europe. She led Crocker on a lengthy tour of the Continent.

When they returned, they placed a $12,000 painting called "The Smoker," by the celebrated French portraitist Meissonier on an easel in the drawing room. Mrs. Crocker's friends stood around the painting and loudly admired the sublimity of expression on the smoker's face. Crocker gazed at the portrait, walked to the back of the room and looked at it, walked up close to it and looked again, and said, "I don't know much about art."

Huntington was nominally the purchasing agent of what was now called the Southern Pacific. He ran the railroad from his office in New York, sending a barrage of telegrams and instructions to agents all over the country. His payroll included nearly the entire Congress of the United States. When the town of Paradise, California, refused to pay what Huntington demanded of it, he rerouted the railroad. That was power.

He didn't need or want a house in San Francisco, since he was rarely there, but his wife was persistent. The solution he found was unusual.

General David Colton was the jovial, somewhat vain business agent of Huntington's in San Francisco. He ran the day-to-day business of the Southern Pacific. The "General" in front of his name was largely an affectation; he had once been a general in the state militia, but had never participated in combat. He had been a friend of Senator Broderick's, and was one of his seconds at the duel. Recognizing his vanity, one of the towns built in the desert had been named after him. That wasn't sufficient; he wanted to be considered as powerful as the Big Four.

Huntington, Crocker, Hopkins and Stanford thought him ludicrous, but they permitted Colton most of the appearances of power. Colton did have good taste, which was rare in those days.

Anxious to impress San Francisco with his prestige, he bought a lot on the summit of Nob Hill and constructed a large and very elegant white Georgian mansion. Then, by a stroke of bad luck, he fell from his horse and was killed.

This was exactly what Huntington needed. Enormous wreaths from the Big Four surrounded Colton's casket. He would have liked this. Then Colton's widow received a sorrowful note from Huntington explaining his surprise and sadness when examining the Southern Pacific's books after her husband's death. There were certain irregularities; it appeared her husband had been rerouting some of the Southern Pacific's assets into his own pocket.

Coming from Huntington, this was especially ludicrous. All of them (Huntington, Stanford, Crocker and Hopkins) siphoned public funds from the treasury at a truly astonishing rate; Huntington had moved the entire Sierra Nevada Mountain range to defraud the Congress. The Colton estate was attached by the courts and handed over to the railroad to make up for the irregularities in the books. Mrs. Huntington, at last, had a mansion on Nob Hill.

By 1880, Nob Hill, capped with Greek temples, medieval castles and baroque cuckoo clocks, was the social Olympus of San Francisco. The Civil War was over; the Shovelry had triumphed over the Chivalry. One by one the southerners abandoned their South Park houses. Even Mrs. Amy Parrott, the queen of the Chivalry, left behind her Grecian bank vault on Rincon Hill and established a house on Nob Hill.

4. THE FRIDAY NIGHT COTILLION SOCIETY

Ned Greenway stated that he would rather see a "female relative of his dead than dragged about the floor in the indecencies of the waltz." . . . Greenway called commands, "Grand right and left," "Royal Arches," "The Basket," and "Reverse Circles."

> Bachelor's Cotillion Club, 1890s,
> from Evelyn Wells' *Champagne
> Days of San Francisco,* 1941.

But Greenway relented:
Such selected buds as Kate Salisbury, Margaret Salisbury and Susie Blanding were permitted the novelty of waltzing to the latest musical rage, "Moonlight and Starlight."

Evelyn Wells, *Champagne Days of San Francisco,* 1941.

On June 4, 1874, twenty-two graying, overweight men in starched shirts and evening clothes sat at the banquet table of the Grand Hotel, listening to a tall, white-bearded man tell stories in a slow southern drawl.

They were the passengers who had sailed into San Francisco Bay on the *Panama* that day twenty-five years earlier. The *Panama* had been scrapped years before, but a keg had been made of some of her timbers and it sat on the table, filled with brandy. Each man sipped some of the brandy. Now that they had completed their ten-course dinner, it was time for speeches.

It was a distinguished audience. It included Judge Hall McAllister and the respected merchant, Sam Ward. A dozen other notables from the passenger list that had produced two senators, three governors, two justices of the United States Supreme Court, an admiral and two generals were present. McAllister was the legal patriarch of San Francisco, living in a brick mansion and honored by his colleagues and friends. He had lost his South Park mansion in a poker game and had been forced to take his family to Europe to avoid the embarrassment that resulted, but now he was firmly back in society. The man speaking was former United States Senator William Gwin, who was reading a telegram of greeting from Jessie Frémont.

John C. Frémont and Jessie were living in a small cottage on Staten Island in New York. His beard was white now. He sat at a rolltop desk and labored at writing his memoirs. Surrounded by old campaign posters, the yellowing journals of his expeditions and tables covered with the souvenirs of his travels, Frémont struggled to justify himself. Jessie quietly wrote articles for magazines and children's stories so they could survive. "I am like a deep-built ship," she said. "I drive best in a strong wind."

Frémont's life, which had always been prone to soar upwards and then, just as suddenly, tumble downwards, had been all downhill since the Civil War. Since their house next to San Francisco Bay had been taken by the army, they had never been properly paid. Their gold mine was long since exhausted. His Civil War service ended ingloriously in a scandal about fraudulent supply contracts. He sank still further after the war when he allowed himself to be tangled in a scandal about fraudulent railroad stock. There were no more mountains to explore, no more snowbound passes to break through. He had been left to selling the use of his name to companies which, more often than not, blamed him when they collapsed. John C. Frémont, "The Pathfinder," was obsolete.

His health began to fail. His doctor advised him to go to California where the climate was healthier. Frémont was too proud to admit he didn't have enough money for the trip. Collis Huntington, learning of Frémont's dilemma, delivered tickets and expense money to Jessie. When Frémont learned of this, he was furious. He went to Huntington's office to return the tickets. Huntington listened, but refused to take the tickets back. "You forget, our road goes over your buried campfires," he said. "I think we rather owe you this."

Frémont and Jessie took the train to Los Angeles where the climate was warmer and drier. They bought a small cottage on Oak Street, but Frémont, as always, refused to sit still. He put on his business suit and traveled to New York as often as he could afford it, trying to salvage something from his shattered business ventures. He was in New York in July 1890, when he was overcome with illness and exhaustion. He died before Jessie could come to him from Los Angeles.

His body was carried to California on one of Huntington's trains. He was buried in Los Angeles in a plain pine box, dressed in a black business suit. Jessie continued to live in the cottage on Oak Street with her daughter until she died two days after Christmas, in 1902.

William Gwin managed to separate himself from the turmoil of the Civil War and return to San Francisco to live. Sadly, he recognized that, because he had picked the wrong side in the war, greater glory was not to be his. Broderick, Green, Howard, and Frémont would have streets named after them; he, who had been one of the state's first senators and the author of its constitution, would not.

He continued to live in their South Park house, watching Mary Bell, in the latest Parisian gown, preside over what was left of the Chivalry. While the party swirled around him, he sat in the corner, quietly playing cribbage.

But he was still interested in politics. In March 1885, he and Mary Bell traveled to Washington once more, to be guests at the inauguration of President Grover Cleveland, the first Democratic president elected since the Civil War. It was a shining moment for Mary Bell Gwin; just as she had entered her ballroom on the eve of the Civil War escorted by President Buchanan, now, twenty-five years later, she entered the Inaugural Ball on the arm of President Cleveland.

For Gwin, the return to Washington had more poignant memories. By himself, he took a carriage to the United States Capitol, and walked slowly through the empty senate chamber where he had sat a quarter of a century earlier. He stopped at his old desk, stood there a few moments in silence, and then walked out of the chamber. Six months later, on a business trip to New York, Gwin died. As he predicted, there were no monuments raised to him in San Francisco.

Lillie Hitchcock returned to San Francisco after the Civil War. Her final sensation at the court of the French

Empire was an appearance at a masked ball in the costume of a San Francisco fireman, complete with red flannel shirt, tightly belted black skirt and fire helmet. She then regaled the Emperor Napoleon with mining camp songs and western dances.

Her return to San Francisco was no less triumphant. Her favorite fire company, Knickerbocker Number Five, read of her exploits in Paris and invited her to their banquet, making her a full member of the fire company. She was presented with a fire helmet and a jeweled numeral five. She wore the number five everywhere.

Her mother was not amused. If she could not have a sedate daughter, she intended to at least have a properly married one. Properly married, of course, meant married to a southerner with money and a job that was not demeaning, that is, a job that didn't require any actual work. Mrs. Hitchcock invited the sons of her southern friends to call on Lillie; they came by the dozen.

But Lillie was nothing if not capricious. She was interested in Howard Coit, a young man she met before going to Paris, who was now chairman of the San Francisco Stock Exchange. Martha Hitchcock disapproved vehemently; there was nothing right about Howard Coit, beginning with the fact that he was from Buffalo, New York. New Yorkers were as popular in the Chivalry's drawing rooms as General Sherman was in Atlanta. Nonetheless, Lillie made a point of meeting Coit as soon as she returned. He was very cool towards her. Since he was the only bachelor in San Francisco who was, Lillie was determined to get him.

Her mother had other ideas. Lillie was promptly sent off to a second exile, this time to the Hitchcocks' country house in Calistoga, a small town seventy-five miles north of the city. Lacking the diversions of San Francisco, Lillie amused herself and startled the tranquil inhabitants of Calistoga by driving a wagon at breakneck speed around the town, drinking prodigious amounts of bourbon and beating the local fast set at poker. At a ball, she met Howard Coit again; this time he wasn't cool to her.

With all the ingenuity of her southern upbringing, Lillie laid out a plot. She arranged to attend a theater matinee in San Francisco with one of her southern suitors. This delighted her mother. Instead of going to the matinee, she eloped with Howard Coit to San Jose. She had only two hours with her new husband before she had to return to San Francisco to take the train to New York with her family. She rushed to the station and boarded the train just as it was about to leave. Since a plot was not fun if anyone else knew about it, she told no one she was married.

The news that San Francisco's most popular young lady had eloped was hard to contain, however. The story hit the San Francisco newspapers while the train was halfway across the country. When they arrived in New York, reporters were waiting on the platform. Lillie admitted to the reporters and to her mortified mother that she was married.

That night, her mother wrote in her diary what might be considered the last words of Chivalry:

"San Francisco is a money-rattling city of nouveaux riches, a panorama of swells who dress to show themselves, feeding their vulgar desire to be seen.... These are the mediocre people who will sink into oblivion within a few years. Lillie, by her marriage to Coit, will also sink into oblivion. She will become one of the Nothing People."

San Francisco's new society had no time to listen to the bitter last words of the outgoing aristocracy. They were discovering what European society had known for centuries: once you had *arrived,* there was nothing left to do. You couldn't go anywhere because you were already *there.* They had lots of money and lots of time and nothing whatsoever to do.

Help came from an unlikely direction, Charles Crocker. Crocker was immensely, totally, thoroughly bored. He was never happy unless he was building something, never content unless he was standing in the sun or rain, shouting at someone or watching someone blow up a mountain or dig a canal for him. He wanted back those days when he had stood at the summit of the Sierras, commanding sixteen thousand men as they burrowed and blasted through the very heart of the mountain. Instead, the railroad kept sending him back to his office, telling him they had enough track and enough canals.

One day Crocker and some Southern Pacific accountants came to the officers of the railroad with a problem. The trains from Monterey, an ocean town over 100 miles south of San Francisco, were nearly always filled going to San Francisco, but on the return, they were nearly empty. How could they fill the trains?

The discussion centered on the East Coast, where the New York Central and Pennsylvania railroads were making a tidy sum carrying fashionable people from New York to the new resorts of Saratoga and Newport. Here they were being entertained at enormous new hotels. This was in imitation of what was happening in Europe. Royalty had long summered or wintered at the Hôtel des Bains on the Lido near Venice. Now, the rage was the hot springs of Baden-Baden in southern Germany. San Francisco emulated this pastime as early as 1856, when some rather smelly hot springs near Napa (a ten-hour boat ride and fifty-mile stagecoach ride north of the city) had been roofed with white frame cottages and a large hotel built nearby. This resort, named White Sulfur Springs after a similar resort in the East, was tremendously popular from the day it opened until the day it burned to the ground. A procession of illustrious people from San Francisco society, led by Mary Bell Gwin, suffered the long journey. Clad in modest ankle-length bathing outfits covered by voluminous skirts, they sat up to their necks in the smelly water. Afterward, they enjoyed the wide veranda of the hotel or took carriage rides through the oak trees around the resort. Each day ended with dancing in the ballroom of the hotel. After a week of this restful life, they braved the stagecoach ride and longer steamboat journey, arriving, exhausted and dusty, in San Francisco, content that they had experienced a little European civilization in the Wild West.

When White Sulfur Springs burned down, a new hotel was built. Soon there were hot springs from Calistoga to Warm Springs, near San Jose, each with its own verandaed hotel. Their advertising brochures claimed the water could cure anything from nearsightedness to tuberculosis.

Charles Crocker was inspired. He had seen the cypress-clad, rocky beaches of Monterey and his wife had taken him to the resort hotels of Italy and Germany. It seemed to him that if a narrow, gritty beach littered with dead fish and seaweed on the Aegean could be an international resort, then surely, the clean white sands of Monterey could support a Western hotel. He determined to build the best resort hotel in the world at Monterey.

For the next hundred days, Charles Crocker could be found not in his office, but sitting in his carriage under a huge tree by the beach at Monterey. Occasionally, he would stand up and yell at the workmen, and then sit back in the carriage, a look of contentment on his face.

The Del Monte Hotel fulfilled all of Crocker's expectations. Not only did it fill the trains going to and from San Francisco to Monterey, but it provided the grandest setting San Francisco Society had ever had in which to do nothing elegantly. Del Monte was San Francisco's Baden-Baden, Hôtel des Bains and Coney Island all in one magnificent place.

In 1880, a good part of San Francisco society rode and sailed to the Del Monte to celebrate its first Fourth of July. Peter Donahue arrived aboard his yacht *Nellie,* Harry Tevis on the *Halcyon,* and the Spreckels brothers, John and Claus, came on their yachts the *Lurline* and the *Relief.* While this colorful flotilla maneuvered offshore, Crocker watched. His daughter Hattie and his son, Colonel Charles Frederick Crocker, rode and drove thoroughbreds from his stable. (In 1888 at the Del Monte, Charles Crocker died. His body was put on a special funeral train that carried it back along his railroad track to San Francisco.)

The train trip from San Francisco took three and one half hours. Dressed in traveling clothes, San Francisco's wealthy gentlemen and their families descended from the train at Monterey accompanied by a retinue of servants and trunks. It was a short drive to the impressive gates of the hotel grounds. A cypress-shaded driveway led to the Hotel Del Monte in all its majesty.

The building was a colossal white confection of balconies and green-shuttered windows, winding stairways and spires with great banners spanking on flagpoles in the brisk ocean breeze. On the shaded veranda, amid rows of white wicker chairs, Ballenberg's Band, dressed in white trousers and blue military tunics, played waltzes. Men wearing white trousers and dark blazers and women in ruffled pastel gowns strolled on the grass between the lawn swings and statues. Some sat at white iron tables under large umbrellas, sipping tea from china teacups. Carriages arrived regularly, dropping newcomers at the door. Society editors from the San Francisco newspapers carefully took note of the arrivals.

There was nothing casual about being casual at the Del Monte. The first evening was devoted to planning one's leisure hours for the coming week. Clothes, with the help of the family maid, were laid out. A different dress, and a different parasol to match it, was required for each day of the visit. In the same way, dress for dinner each evening, gowns for the nightly dances, and tennis and bathing costumes had to be planned.

After breakfast in the enormous white dining room, relaxation began in earnest. The men mainly retired to the dark-paneled bar (no women were allowed), and spent much of the day quietly drinking, talking and playing cards. The women went on excursions run by the hotel. These were announced on large placards in the lobby. There were carriage trips along the beach, carriage trips through the cypress groves, and carriage trips a few miles south to see the old Spanish mission of Carmel. The mission was abandoned and crumbling away, but no one gave any thought to trying to save it; indeed, they would have been appalled by the thought. Gazing at ruined buildings was considered to be a sublime experience. The Carmel mission was one of the very few ruins California was privileged to have.

The carriages returned by ten in the morning, when the swimming began. There were several heated salt-water bathing tanks on the grounds of the hotel, each warmed to a different temperature. The women began appearing shortly after ten, dressed in their bathing costumes, gray blouses and ankle-length skirts over bloomers and stockings.

Proper women disapproved of the young women wearing Parisian bathing costumes—striped tights that made them look like circus performers.

Each bathing tank was divided by a net designed to keep women on one side and men on the other. As the more conservative San Francisco newspapers observed disapprovingly, the nets were frequently removed and men and women intermingled in the bathing tank.

After the morning swim, the guests returned to their rooms to change for the midday meal in the dining room. Leisurely outdoor activities were saved for the afternoons, among them: lawn bowling, tennis, croquet, and walks among the trees and on the beach. For the less athletic, there were card games, elevating lectures on the spiritual qualities of art and literature, or amateur dramatics. One could also simply sit on the porch and listen to Ballenberg's Band play waltzes. There was an endless repertoire of waltzes.

The men emerged from the bar around dinnertime, and the whole family dined in the huge dining hall, surrounded by black-tuxedoed waiters. After dinner the men retreated to the bar and the women retreated to their rooms to rest and change for the dance. When they came downstairs again around nine o'clock, Ballenberg's

Band had changed from their white trousers and military tunics into black evening dress, and were in the ballroom, playing waltzes.

For the young people, the dance was the most interesting part of their stay at the Del Monte. Here was where the flirtation went on, and, regardless of what the hotel brochures said, that was far more exciting than looking at cypress trees or a ruined Spanish mission. For the young women in the 1880s, the United States Navy provided an additional benefit; military duties were not permitted to interfere with the officers' social lives. This meant that all naval maneuvers were held within a short launch ride of a good hotel. Ships of the United States Navy anchored frequently at Monterey, conveniently close to the Del Monte Hotel. The ballroom was filled each night with young navy officers in starched blue uniforms and crisp gold braid.

Thus, what appeared ordinary to their elders (who yawned and tapped their feet in time with Ballenberg's Band) was, for the young people, an enchanted carnival of romance and intrigue.

In the romantic 1880s, nothing was done directly. A few words would never do when an elaborate note, preferably perfumed and, better yet, written in a bizarre secret code, could be sent. Everything, in fact, was done in code. There was a glove code, a fan code and a handkerchief code. Pulling the handkerchief across the lips meant, "I am desirous of making further acquaintance"; across the cheek, "I love you"; flick the handkerchief over the shoulder, "Follow me"; wound around the forefinger, "I am engaged"; wound around the third finger, "I am married"; bite the handkerchief, "I am angry with you"; touch the right eye with the handkerchief, "Mama is looking."

Thus, as the dancing went on for hour after hour, the elders overlooked, or pretended to overlook, a veritable blizzard of fan waving, glove dropping, glove tugging, handkerchief wiping, twisting and poking as messages flashed around the room. It was all grand fun.

Yet even at the Del Monte, there was a feeling that something was missing. Society should have been content. They had money, enormous houses, suits from London, gowns from Italy and stuffed hummingbirds on their blouses every bit as ridiculous-looking as the ones being worn that season in Paris. They could misquote Oscar Wilde as well as any New Yorker and, while their genealogies were perhaps not as long, their children had as many middle names as any French marquis or Austrian archduke. What was missing?

They realized it was a sense of exclusiveness. As they looked around the Del Monte ballroom at the men in starched white shirts and black coats with diamond pins and gold watch chains and women in silk gowns, diamond tiaras and sapphire dog collars, they felt a sensation of uneasiness. One knew that the Gwins, Crockers, Tevises, Haggins, Floods, McAllisters and others were society, but what of the others? A woman in the corner, dressed from head to foot in rubies and ostrich feathers, might be a Crocker or an upstairs maid who had stock in a silver mine. She could even be the madam of a Barbary Coast bordello, who had switched to real estate manipulation. The stately-looking man with his thumbs tucked in his vest might be a banker or someone who won his fortune the night before in a Pacific Street poker game.

It was all terribly uncertain. At the swimming tank, where you couldn't count the other person's diamonds, it was even worse. The worst thing was that, while you were looking at other people and wondering, a Crocker or a Flood might be looking at you and wondering.

A champagne salesman named Ned Greenway saved San Francisco society from this dilemma.

The plump, short Greenway wore an immense handlebar mustache. Day or night, he wore evening clothes. He strutted from ballroom to salon with the authority of a Prussian field marshal, which in fact, he rather resembled. When he danced, he sprang to his toes and floated around the room like a balloon.

His capacity for champagne was truly amazing; he boasted that he had drunk twenty-five bottles in one day. "I have drunk more wine than any man in America," he said proudly. "I can tell you the year and brand of any champagne by tasting it blindfolded." In fact, his only break from drinking champagne during the course of an evening was when he rested his palate with a few glasses of beer. When his weight bothered him, he kept on drinking champagne but stopped eating anything other than lady fingers and pickled limes, which he considered a gentleman's diet.

Greenway's position in society rested solely on the fact that he knew the right way to do everything, from selecting champagne to introducing oneself to the Archbishop of Canterbury—should the occasion arise. He knew precisely how to walk, dress, yawn, lean over, take a fish bone from one's mouth; he could even eat corn on the cob with dignity, which is no easy feat. He knew when to insert French in his conversation, and he could pronounce the items on a French menu with an accent and enthusiasm that was awesome. Because of these skills his advice and presence was sought by every hostess in San Francisco.

Greenway came to San Francisco from Baltimore in the mid-1870s. He was twenty-two. He carried letters of introduction as the new West Coast representative of Mumm's Champagne. Before long, he was a fixture in the Gwins' salon; soon he was seen in every fashionable place in town. He sang in amateur operas and appeared in benefit theatricals, and he was a regular guest at the Del Monte Hotel. There were even rumors of an engagement to James Flood's daughter Jennie. He fit in wherever he went. Social events became incomplete without Greenway. His energy was truly remarkable; habitually he danced all night and slept until four in the afternoon. Once, when he was disturbed from this schedule by a morning appointment and was having breakfast at the Palace Hotel, the waiter asked him, "How are you feeling this morning, Mr. Greenway?" "A gentleman never feels well in the morning," Greenway growled.

By 1887 he had arrived. A charter member of society, his name headed every invitation list. But he, like the people in the ballroom of the Del Monte Hotel, felt there was still too much uncertainty. He had worked hard, drunk a lot of champagne and answered a lot of foolish questions to get where he was; he wanted to be certain that where he was, was someplace exclusive.

Greenway and the rest of San Francisco society faithfully read the society news from New York, the source of all social wisdom and propriety. The comings and goings of the Vanderbilts and Astors were enviously followed. Ward McAllister, Hall McAllister's brother, had, with the aid of Mrs. Astor, the "Mystic Rose," neatly divided

New York society into the *ins* and the *outs* by the simple expedient of drawing up a list of only those socially elect who could be accommodated in the Astors' New York ballroom. This list became known as New York's "Four Hundred." No position in society was more eagerly sought or so jealously guarded. The idea appealed to Greenway who thought he was certainly as qualified as Ward McAllister to write such a list. All he needed was a "Mystic Rose" to give it authority.

To be San Francisco's "Mystic Rose," Greenway chose Mrs. Eleanor Martin. No woman in San Francisco could approach either the awesome respectability or the physical size of Mrs. Eleanor Martin. She sailed through San Francisco society with the serene authority of a battleship. Her home was a fortress of respectability; divorced women were not permitted and any young lady who accepted more than a glass of champagne was not invited again. Her dinner parties were solemn. Matters discussed at her table were of such gravity that Mrs. Martin frequently dozed and had to be supported lest she fall forward into the asparagus.

She could, and often did, trace her ancestry back through the Founding Fathers into remote antiquity. More recently, she could claim to be the sister of a former governor and the sister-in-law of Peter Donahue, the founder of the San Francisco Gas Works and a man of great social weight. Her sister, Anna Downey Donahue, emphasized her social position by riding through Golden Gate Park every Sunday in a glass coach. In short, Mrs. Martin's place in society was as solid and unmoving as bedrock.

When Greenway approached her with the idea of a Bachelors' Cotillion, she was delighted. The two of them sat down with great enthusiasm to make a list of who should belong in San Francisco society.

Their criteria were arbitrary. If you were part of the old Chivalry, and a friend of Mrs. Martin, you were *in*. If your last name was Crocker, Haggin, Tevis, Flood or another of a dozen gilded names, you were *in*. If, over the years, you bought large quantities of Mumm's Extra Dry Champagne, it didn't hurt. Otherwise, you had to hope you had never inadvertently offended either Greenway or Mrs. Martin, who had notably long memories.

The chosen ones received in the mail their certificate of membership in society. This beautifully engraved card invited them to attend five dances, from ten P.M. until three A.M., to be held at the Odd Fellows Hall following a supper at the home of Mrs. Eleanor Martin. The delighted condescension of those who received invitations and the anguish of those who didn't (and frantically checked their mail each morning, hoping their invitation had somehow been delayed) can only be imagined.

Then the preparations began. For the women of 1887, this, of course, meant skin-tight, low-cut, satin gowns decorated with ribbons. Long buttoned gloves, a feather boa and a fur muff were considered essential. Hair was worn in an elaborate knot, to complement diamond earrings and a diamond choker which fit snugly into what were called "Venus rings," the doubled flesh under the chin. Fat was very fashionable.

On the chosen evening, the young lady, suitably gowned, boaed, and bedecked with the most and the best jewels her family could assemble, was delivered to the door of the Martin house. Here, a butler announced her name. After shaking hands with the awesome Mrs. Martin, she was guided to a long, formidably laden table.

Frozen with terror, one sat through the dinner, smiling weakly lest some error displease Mrs. Martin and lead to permanent banishment from her house. Mrs. Martin seemed oblivious to this; in fact, she seemed asleep.

Shortly after nine o'clock, the table was cleared. Guests stammered their gratitude to Mrs. Martin as they were ushered into carriages to take them to the Odd Fellows Hall.

At the hall, they were led through the murmuring army of chaperones and handed their cotillion favors. The men were given handpainted pocketbooks or odd keychains. The women received painted paper fans or miniature rhinestoned canoe paddles. Presumably, these favors were taken home and placed in a drawer to be treasured for years. With their favors, boas and muffs safely deposited in the cloakroom, they lined up to wait.

At precisely ten o'clock, Ballenberg's Band thundered into "The Blue Danube" waltz. Mrs. Martin appeared on one side of the ballroom, while Ned Greenway, in superbly tailored evening dress, appeared on the other. The enormous Mrs. Martin, glittering with jewels, advanced toward the dapper Greenway, each stepping to the music, until they reached the center of the room. Greenway bowed deeply over Mrs. Martin's outstretched hand, kissed it, and with linked arms they began the promenade around the ballroom. At a strategic corner of the ballroom, Greenway stopped, pulled a small gold whistle from his pocket, and blew a shrill blast. This was the signal for the dancing to begin.

The dancing was not precisely dancing, as we usually use the word; it was more like military drill. Greenway and Mrs. Martin led the guests in a rigorous march up and down the ballroom, turning, wheeling and executing complicated steps that would bewilder a ballerina. He called out commands: "Grand Right, Grand Left!" "Royal Arches!" "Reversed Circle!" Each command was articulated by a short toot on his whistle.

After two hours of this, Greenway blew his whistle to indicate it was time to eat. The exhausted dancers rushed to tables laden with terrapin, scalloped oysters, ham, tongue, duck, ice cream and, of course, Mumm's Extra Dry Champagne. They had to hurry, for Greenway was a strict cotillion master. He soon had them back on the floor executing the dance figures again. Finally, at three in the morning, when Greenway gave a final toot on his whistle, it came to an end. Ballenberg's Band stopped playing; the guests applauded; Greenway bowed. Tired, but happy, the selected collected their feather boas and favors and boarded carriages for the ride home.

Needless to say, the success of Greenway's Friday night cotillion caused a great deal of jealousy. Soon there was competition.

William Chambliss dressed and carried himself with great authority. He had come from Mississippi and had been an officer on a steamship, a position (he thought) of no little prestige. Furthermore, he could trace his ancestry in greater detail and farther back than even Mrs. Martin—which was no small feat. When the San Francisco *Chronicle* announced that it had chosen Ned Greenway to write a column of social commentary, the San Francisco *Examiner* turned to William Chambliss.

The only way to compete with an exclusive society is to form an even more exclusive society. Chambliss did. He formed the Monday night Evening Club which, he announced, was the only genuine society in San Francisco. He even took a subtle swipe at Greenway, intimating he was one of the "self-elected leaders and dictators of so-called social clubs who claim that a little money and a few false notices in the third-rate newspapers give high social rating to all the saloon keepers, gamblers, sports and prize fighters who attend their money-making functions," and should be "relegated without unnecessary delay to the ranks of colored society." If it seems from this that Chambliss was bigoted toward blacks, it should in fairness be pointed out that he was equally bigoted toward the Chinese, the Japanese, anyone of Latin American descent, and most Europeans. "What we sorely need is a European exclusion act that will shut out foreign immigration of all classes," he pronounced.

Despite these spirited attacks, Greenway's club continued to dominate the social calendar. Chambliss deserted the *Examiner* and began to publish "Chambliss' Weekly," his own social journal with his picture on the cover. Among other things, this weekly warned gentlemen that they were not gentlemen if they did not wear white gloves at all times. The paper did not prosper.

Chambliss' personal fortunes, which were tied to a novel plan to rent out advertising space on the ceilings of barbershops, were also not prospering. Chambliss poured his fury into a book, which, he announced, would shake San Francisco society into the Bay. It was called *Chambliss' Diary* or *Society as It Really Is.*

It began by describing, at great length, Chambliss' ancestry. Then it described how Chambliss, when he first arrived in San Francisco, cleverly exposed the young men of society as gamblers by losing several thousand dollars to them in a poker game. From there it proceeded to define "the Parvenucracy," that is, anyone who made the fortune Chambliss thought he should have made. Every scandal, hint of scandal and breath of a hint of scandal that could be construed was mentioned. The Crocker family were accused of having Indian blood. There were not enough bad things to say about Greenway. He even took swings at his old employer, the *Examiner*. The Del Monte Hotel was described as "a hot-bed for scandal . . ." where the Parvenucracy and doveshooters go and where young "society ladies" go into the gentlemen's bathing tank in a seminude state in order to see their pictures published in the *Examiner*. Before he was finished, he had hurled mud at everyone in town.

Surprisingly, he had trouble finding a publisher. He claimed the families he had exposed paid off the local publishing companies to keep the book out of print. Using a printer in New York, he published it himself. When the book finally did appear, it caused a minor sensation. For a short time many of the families mentioned in it bought up quantities of the book which they burned. The furor quickly died down. The people who most wanted to read the book, the housewives and clerks who aspired to society, wanted to read gossip. Instead, they read Chambliss' scornful putting down of people who had once been housewives and clerks. The sales of the book died, and Chambliss rapidly faded from San Francisco's eye. Greenway's position was secure.

5. HEARST, de YOUNG AND THE DIVINE SARAH

In December 1878 San Francisco was treated to the greatest craze in theater: Gilbert and Sullivan.

Determined to outshine New York, San Francisco's millionaires built the largest and most pretentious theaters money could buy. William Ralston opened the California Theater in 1869. Stanford, Fair, Flood, Mackay and even the looney Emperor Norton were in attendance at this enormous, marble-floored, gaslit palace on opening night. In 1876, "Lucky" Baldwin opened a theater inside his new hotel. Baldwin claimed the gilt, red plush, satin curtains and crystal chandeliers "had no rival, even in art-loving Europe." Drawn by huge salaries, the most famous actors in America came to play on these stages. Edwin Booth, Helen Modjeska, Maude Adams, James Murdoch, James McCulloch and a dozen others entertained San Francisco.

In the boxes and dress circles, a diamonded, white-tied,

Parisian-gowned society could leave behind business, divorce, and scandal for a few hours. This was their place; New York could do no better.

San Francisco demanded not only the greatest actors, but also the newest plays. When they learned of the Gilbert and Sullivan craze in England, agents were dispatched to the East to bring them to San Francisco. Unable to obtain the legal rights from Gilbert and Sullivan, they set out to steal the plays. When *H.M.S. Pinafore* opened in London in 1878, stenographers in the balcony clandestinely took down the dialogue, while stagehands were bribed to steal the music from the orchestra pit. Days after *Pinafore* opened in London, a pirate version was on stage in New York. By Christmas Eve, 1878, *H.M.S. Pinafore* opened in San Francisco to a packed house.

Unfortunately, the stenographers who took down the dialogue in London forgot to note that *H.M.S. Pinafore* was a comedy, so the actors performed it as a drama of the sea. The program in San Francisco announced, "A real ship mounted with real sailors! Real cannon! A realistic production!" Dramatic nautical music and authentic sea chanteys were added where managers thought them appropriate. At the end of the performance, the audience left the theater shaking their heads.

In January 1865, the popularity of the theater caused the de Young brothers to start the San Francisco *Daily Dramatic Chronicle,* a review of current plays. Charles and his brother Michael, who had come to San Francisco from St. Louis as children in 1850, handed out seven thousand free copies of their first issue. After they found they were able to sell it, they added local news and Charles wrote violent political editorials. With "Daily" and "Dramatic" dropped, the *Chronicle* became the leading newspaper in San Francisco.

The *Chronicle* offered generous portions of scandal and outrage, as did every San Francisco newspaper. What made the *Chronicle* popular was the extreme vehemence of the editorials Charles de Young wrote. He never let an opponent off as a "scoundrel" or a "thief" if he could be called a "degenerate, skulking, vile, foul, depraved sewer creature," or something stronger.

In 1880 de Young unleashed his vocabulary against a Baptist minister and politician named Isaac Kalloch, who was running for mayor. Kalloch replied with unkind and un-Baptist words for de Young. In response, de Young hopped in his carriage, drove to Kalloch's church and shot the minister in the leg. He was jailed for a day and fined. Charles de Young continued his assault on Kalloch. The latter's son retaliated by invading the *Chronicle* office and murdering the editor.

Since there were no bodyguards in those days, there was always the chance that an editorial would provoke someone enough to shoot the editor. This happened in the 1850s, when James King of William (he used this unusual name to distinguish himself from another James King in the city), the editor of the *Evening Bulletin,* was shot on the street by a county supervisor whom he attacked in an editorial. In the ensuing confusion, a Vigilance Committee was formed, the city government was temporarily overthrown and the supervisor was hanged by the vigilantes. San Francisco journalism was never dull, and it always made fascinating copy for Eastern papers.

Michael de Young took over after his brother's death. Although his editorials were milder than Charles', he managed to provoke Adolph B. Spreckels, the son of the man who won part of the Hawaiian Islands in a poker game. Spreckels stormed into Michael de Young's office and tried to repeat what Kalloch's son had done. Luckily for de Young, Spreckels was a terrible shot. He managed to shoot the desk, the draperies, the windows and the lamps—but not de Young—before he was dragged from the office.

As long as the people you wrote editorials about were poor shots, journalism was an exciting profession. It was a profession that attracted a colorful assortment of men and women. One of these, a tall, lumbering youth with perpetually mussed hair, innocent blue eyes and the awkward, but somehow charming manners of a benign polar bear, was named William Randolph Hearst.

His father, George Hearst, left a farm in Missouri to come to San Francisco in 1850. Like everyone else, Hearst invested in gold mine stock; unlike everyone else, he invested in the right gold mine stock, the Homestake Mine in South Dakota. In a short time, he had several hundred million dollars. Like everyone else, he turned to silver, and then to copper. Once more, he picked the right stock, that of the Anaconda Mine in Montana. Several hundred million dollars piled onto his first fortune. He bought real estate, mines in South America, ranch land in Mexico, and a failing newspaper in San Francisco called the *Examiner*.

He also acquired a wife, Phoebe, and a son, William, whom his wife spoiled terribly.

When he reached the proper age, William was sent to Harvard. Before his abundant sense of humor got him expelled, William dashed to New York to see every new play, wrote frequent letters to his mother asking for more money and acquired a taste for journalism working as business agent for one of the student publications. When he returned to San Francisco he asked his father for the *Examiner*. His father had some doubts about the respectability of journalists, but gave in and presented the paper to William, who was twenty-four years old.

On March 6, 1887, a small notice in the staff box announced, "The *Examiner*, with this issue, has become the exclusive property of William Randolph Hearst, the son of its former proprietor." The headline that day expanded poetically on a previous day's story: DEAD BABIES: BLOODY WORK: MORE GHASTLY LIGHT ON THE SLAUGHTER OF THE INNOCENTS: THE DARK MYSTERIES OF A GREAT CITY.

Young Hearst, who loved the theater, was determined that the news should be at least as dramatic and exciting as his favorite plays. He set out to find men who shared this idea. A tall, blond Scotsman named Arthur McEwen was hired as the new editor. McEwen was asked what his definition of news was. He replied that the reader, when he saw the first page of the paper, should say "Gee Whiz!"; when he turned to the second page, he should exclaim "Holy Moses!"; when he reached the third page, he should shriek, "God Almighty!" Hearst liked that.

Hearst then hired the acid-penned Ambrose Bierce to write a weekly column. Bierce chose as his first theme the Western Art Show, which was then on display in the city. He opened his column by cheerfully calling the art critic of the rival *Bulletin* a "smirking idiot" and an "anile and unhaired wretch." Then he went on to describe the art show, whose quality, he wrote, "while always detestable, has this year attained a shining pinnacle of badness. The pictures next year will necessarily be better than the pictures of this, but alas, there may be more of them." Hearst liked that.

But despite his new staff, two weeks later Hearst found himself badly scooped. The Del Monte Hotel burned down, and the *Chronicle* had the story first.

Hearst was determined to try to salvage something from the story. He hired a locomotive, sent his reporters to the station, and within an hour of the *Chronicle* story he had an *Examiner* special train hurtling to Monterey to interview the witnesses and draw pictures of the ruins.

The next day the headlines on the front page of the *Examiner* screamed,

HUNGRY, FRANTIC FLAMES!
THEY LEAP MADLY UPON THE SPLENDID PLEASURE
   PALACE
BY THE BAY OF MONTEREY
ENCIRCLING DEL MONTE IN THEIR RAVENOUS
   EMBRACE
FROM PINNACLE TO FOUNDATION
'LEAPING HIGHER, HIGHER, HIGHER,
   WITH DESPERATE DESIRE!'

While this was fascinating, it wasn't especially news. The *Chronicle* had reported the news the day before. Hearst's grand idea was to make his train, not the fire, the star of the story.

"Drawn up at the platform, panting with madness to be free, was the huge locomotive, the mightiest, stoutest engine on the road. . . . The engineer, a tried and famous veteran in his line, stood with the lever in his sinewly grasp, like a weather-beaten captain at the ship's helm. . . .

"As leaps the arrow from the bow or as the rocket spurns the earth, so the meteor-like bullet of steam and steel pierced the cold morning air, quivering and shrieking as it sped. . . .

"The chariot of fire moving through space to meet the sweeping whirlwind; a very whirling, blustering, rumbling tempest. . . .

"As the larger towns were reached, the excited inhabitants crowded from their houses to hail the speeding train and shout their acclaims for the *Examiner*'s enterprise.

" 'Are the wires down?' asked one gentleman.

" 'No, but they are not sufficient,' was the reply."

What news did this desperate enterprise gather? Almost none. The *Chronicle* had already printed the details of the fire, and the best the *Examiner*'s trainload of reporters could get was an eyewitness account of "scantily-adorned beauties" fleeing the flaming hotel. But Hearst was delighted to find that he was selling as many copies of his paper as the *Chronicle* was of its. People were fascinated by the story of his special train. He had discovered what was to be his most profitable journalistic rule; when there isn't any news, send someone to make some.

Each day the *Examiner* reported a new drama, a new adventure, or another hair-raising escape. On days when the news was slow, *Examiner* reporters were commanded to jump into the Bay to see how long it would take before they were rescued, or to feign seizures to see if anyone would help them. These stories were written. The headlines were always blood-curdling:

EATEN BY SHARKS
SAD ENDING TO A DAY'S PLEASURE

or, after some frightened cows stampeded and chased some picnickers from their pasture:

BOVINE TERRORS

FAMILY COWS GO MAD

"...The fiery, warlike bovine had scattered a hundred men in a few seconds ... the cow was in the act of running her through with her horns when assistance arrived...."

During this time, William Randolph Hearst noticed a small item in his paper. Sarah Bernhardt, the greatest actress in the world, was in New York. Reading further, Hearst learned that she had acted in a play called *Fedora,* which had been written especially for her, at the Star Theater. Even though her lines were in French, a language few in the audience understood, they rose en masse and fairly screamed at the end of the third act. She was recalled three times. The audiences shouted and hammered their hands on the sides of the boxes. She was deluged with flowers; one floral display took eight men to carry onstage.

Hearst (and all the rest of the world) knew the stories about Sarah Bernhardt. "The Divine Sarah" was barely five feet tall, but her eyes could pierce the eyes of a man in the very back row. Her voice, which could rise from a whisper to a terrible shout, could make the whole theater tremble. She never performed the part of Camille without moving everyone in the house to tears, even if they didn't understand French.

Hearst knew something else; she was scheduled to come to San Francisco. If there was any person in the world whose life fit William Randolph Hearst's notions of what a life should be, it was Sarah Bernhardt. He resolved to have her for the San Francisco *Examiner*.

On Friday, May 13, 1887, a special train steamed into the tiny town of Humboldt, Nevada, and clanked to a stop. Several blanketed Indians stood silently on the platform. Near them stood Sam Davis, a reporter for the Associated Press, the Carson *Appeal* and the San Francisco *Examiner*.

Sam Davis eyed a car with the name "Sarah Bernhardt" lettered in gold on the side. Through the window, he could see a table covered with empty breakfast dishes, a champagne bottle, and a chess board with the pieces knocked over. Behind it was the unmistakable profile of Sarah Bernhardt.

While the rest of the company went into the Railway Hotel for lunch, Davis sought out Bernhardt's manager in the car behind hers. The manager was surprised to see a reporter in the middle of Nevada, and agreed to arrange an interview with Miss Bernhardt. He returned a few moments later; the actress wanted to be alone for an hour, but she would see him.

At the end of an hour, the manager led Davis through the door of the "Sarah Bernhardt." She sat alone in the middle of the car, wearing a silver sheath. As he approached, she rose majestically and extended her left hand. She began speaking in French.

"How I like this country," she said. "It is a cold country, but there is electricity in the air. I feel it in my arms." She drew out her hair with her fingers.

When the conversation turned to San Francisco, it became evident why Hearst had chosen Sam Davis. He knew precisely what would appeal to Bernhardt's sense of the romantic. He began describing the exotic cos-

87

tumes, dark alleys, underground passageways and opium
dens of Chinatown. Bernhardt listened, enchanted. She
insisted that she be taken to Chinatown when she came
to San Francisco. She turned herself over to the San
Francisco *Examiner.* Hearst's plan had succeeded.

The next morning, when she stepped off the train at
Port Costa for the ferry to San Francisco, Sam Davis
was waiting for her with a copy of that morning's
Examiner. As the other actresses milled about the fer-
ryboat, wearing live beetles bound to their jackets by
tiny golden chains (the latest Paris fashion), Bernhardt
eagerly turned the pages of the paper. There were not
only pictures of her, but pictures of two of her sculptures, "Death and the Maiden" and "The Drowned Son."
Hearst knew exactly how to appeal to her vanity.
Bernhardt, her eyes shining, turned to Davis and kissed
him, first on the right cheek, then the left cheek, and on
the lips.

"The right cheek for the *Appeal,*" she said, "the left
cheek for the *Examiner,* and the lips, my dear friend, for
yourself."

Davis grinned. "Madame," he said, "I also represent
the Associated Press, which serves three hundred and
eighty papers west of the Mississippi."

Bernhardt was met at the Palace Hotel by several
carriage-loads of *Examiner* reporters, detectives, and
translators. She was driven to the Chinese Theater,
where she startled the audience by impulsively walking
onstage to question the actors.

Her entourage led her through a narrow alley, into a
dark courtyard, and down a steep flight of steps into an
opium den. By the light of the single candle in the room,
they saw bunks full of men, their eyes glazed.

"C'est magnifique!" Bernhardt sighed.

When *Fedora* opened at the Baldwin Theater the following night, all San Francisco society was there. James Haggin and Lloyd Tevis sat with their wives in the first proscenium box. Tevis's wife wore a satin dress with a white Chinese shawl. John Mackay and Lillie Coit sat in the next box. Mrs. Baldwin was next to them. Mrs. James Fair and her daughter Tessie, wearing a bonnet sprayed with wild flowers, sat in another box. Henry Crocker, Jr., Hall McAllister, the Baron von Schroeder, Harry Tevis and Mrs. Fred Sharon sat in other boxes around the proscenium. Below, in the dress circle, were Adolph Spreckels, Michael de Young and Mrs. de Young. The latter flouted convention by not wearing a bonnet; her hair was set in a Greek style.

There was more to talk about than Mrs. de Young's hairstyle, however. By now everyone knew that Bernhardt had breakfasted at the home of William H. Crocker. This revelation shocked because Bernhardt was divorced, and no divorcée was permitted to enter a house on Nob Hill. For now, she would be forgiven. Sin was expected of artists.

When the curtain fell at the end of the first act with Bernhardt weeping over her dead husband, the audience burst into applause and called her back three times. At the end of the play, when she stood alone in front of the curtain, the audience rose to its feet, shouting. Roses pattered onto the stage all around her until it looked as if she stood on a red carpet.

Society, in the front rows and boxes, was on its feet applauding and shouting. When they could, they shouted in French. "Artiste incomparable!" "Magnifique!" If they didn't know French, they shouted what they could. The

89

theater rang with cries of "Mon Dieu!" "Au Revoir!" and "Filet of sole!" The *Examiner* critic reported that Michael de Young of the *Chronicle* was madly looking through a French dictionary. Bernhardt was called back onstage six times before the audience let her go.

6. TITLE HUNTING

The mountains of California gave San Francisco's elite nearly everything they wanted: houses as large as railroad stations, armies of servants, diamonds as big as strawberries, private railway cars, carriages bearing their family crests and performances by Sarah Bernhardt, but they could not give them the one thing they really wanted, acceptance in New York. An invitation to Greenway's Cotillion was a great thing in San Francisco, but it could not get one into the Astors' ballroom in New York, and that was the place that counted. No matter how much wealth they had amassed, no matter how many old masters hung in their living rooms, San Francisco's elite were still treated shabbily in New York.

Easterners believed that San Francisco was still a Wild West mining camp. When the Duke of Manchester visited San Francisco, he was entertained at the home of the Milton Lathams. Latham and his friends, dressed in formal evening clothes and gowns, were startled when the duke appeared in boots and a red flannel shirt. He apologized and confessed that all he knew about the West was what he had read in Bret Harte's stories.

A story, widely circulated in the East, was that when the French government sent the San Francisco Art Association a copy of the Venus de Milo, the Art Association sued Wells Fargo for damages because the arms were missing. Wells Fargo, the story went, paid in full.

What particularly galled the Floods, Mackays, Crockers and other members of the Golden Circle was that they, who collectively had enough money to buy most, if not all, of New York state, were denied entrance to the Astor ballroom. Even the most threadbare and impoverished Bavarian prince or Italian contessa was granted instant entry. The great irony of the nineteenth and, for that matter, the twentieth century was that nowhere is a title held in more respect and awe than in democratic America.

The men didn't particularly care (or pretended they didn't), but the women did. They wanted their daughters to be as respected as any Astor or Vanderbilt. If that meant they had to have a title, then they would get them a title.

Fortunately, a recent flurry of revolutions and uprisings had left Europe filled with unemployed barons and landless dukes languishing in run-down hotels.

Rules of protocol reserved titles, such as empress of Austria or queen of England, for nationals, but a surprising variety of other titles was available. Each capital in Europe had at least a dozen nobles of some sort who had dress uniforms, rows of medals and a willingness to marry Americans who could support them in the way they had once been accustomed. The Ritz, Grand and Sacher Hotels were soon crowded with young American heiresses and their mothers, shopping for titles.

The practice was first made fashionable by (of course, a New Yorker) Jennie Jerome. She married Lord Randolph Churchill, who received her two-hundred-thousand-dollar dowry in 1874. The marriage was not only reasonably happy, it also resulted in the birth of Winston Churchill.

San Francisco kept up. In 1880 Sir Thomas George Fermor-Hesketh sailed into San Francisco Bay aboard his steam yacht *Lancashire Witch*. A not particularly attractive man who was getting old, he stepped ashore at the dock of the San Francisco Yacht Club, and took a coach to the Palace Hotel. Without his crested blazer, he would have looked like a retired accountant or druggist, but when he was announced as the seventh baronet of Lancaster, he took on (in San Francisco's eyes) the armor and heraldry of a Lancelot. One newspaper described him as "the best specimen of a thoroughbred Englishman who ever visited California," as if he were a prize horse.

Sir Thomas, it was explained, was making a leisurely tour of the world and had just come from the Del Monte Hotel. It was more than likely he had come to San Francisco to do more than look at redwood trees. As he rode the new hydraulic elevator of the Palace Hotel, his eyes caught those of a pretty young lady in the elevator and her eyes caught his. Her eyes probably would not have stayed on his for long had she not known that he was the seventh baronet of Lancaster—but that is conjecture. The young lady, Flora Sharon, was the daughter of William Sharon, the owner of the Palace Hotel.

When he left the elevator, Sir Thomas made inquiries about the young lady. Her father (noting who Sir Thomas was) arranged an introduction as quickly as possible. After the payment of a dowry of almost five million dollars, Flora Sharon became Lady Hesketh. The two sailed away aboard the *Lancashire Witch* for their estates at Easton, Neston and Somerville, hopefully, as the newspapers said, to live happily ever after.

The title race was on. Anna Downey Donahue (whose sister was Mrs. Eleanor Martin, and whose husband was the founder of the San Francisco Gas Works and owner of San Francisco's only glass coach) was determined that her daughter Mary Ellen would have a title. After a deliberate search, an appropriate noble was found. In December 1883 Mary Ellen was wed to Baron Henry von Schroeder. The baron played his part splendidly, clicking his heels and wearing the iron cross which had been presented to him by Field Marshal von Moltke during the recent Franco-Prussian War.

The Crockers got in on the act with the marriage of Mrs. William Henry Crocker's sister, Beth Sperry of Stockton, to Prince André Poniatowski, a descendent of the last king of Poland. There was much gossip about the intermarriage of Polish and American Indian blood (which was said to be in the Sperry family), but the marriage prospered. Backed by his brother-in-law, Poniatowski (whose nickname was "Pony-of-Whiskey") made a success of a racetrack at Tanforan. Eventually, he and his American wife moved to Paris, but their descendants returned to California and settled in Santa

Barbara. There were several daughters in the fourth generation. Every now and then, San Franciscans not up on their genealogy would note with surprise that a girl with a strange Polish name was making her debut at the Cotillion.

Collis Huntington's adopted daughter, Clara Prentice Huntington, approached her father, begging him to get her a title. Huntington, who spent nearly all his time in his tiny New York office sitting behind a huge heap of papers and wearing a black skullcap, was not delighted by the idea. He was having his own difficulties with the railroad. David Colton's widow wanted her house back. As part of her lawsuit, she published letters between Huntington and her late husband which showed in embarrassing detail how Huntington had bought the entire state legislature of California. The newspapers in San Francisco were crusading against him. The *Examiner,* in some of its milder criticism, said he had "the soul of a shark." Secondly, Huntington was loath to give away money. Once, he found a twenty-five-cent error in a hotel bill and told the clerk, "Young man, you can't follow me through life by the quarters I've dropped."

Criticism did not bother Huntington, who was used to it, but it did bother Clara. She became even more determined to escape the sordidness of business and politics by rising above it to what she imagined was the fairy-tale majesty of the life of royalty. Finally, Huntington relented and found a prince for Clara. He paid a dowry of five million dollars and she became (just what she wanted) the Princess von Hatzfeld-Wildenberg.

Eva Julia Bryant Mackay wanted a prince, too—especially since Clara Huntington had gotten one. Her mother, the former Louise Hungerford Bryant, agreed.

Mrs. Mackay and Eva (the surviving daughter of her first marriage to a Virginia City doctor who died prematurely) let it be known that they were bored with San Francisco society. Whenever possible, Mrs. Mackay left her husband behind and traveled with Eva to London and Paris. There, the mother and daughter, wearing sapphires the size of pigeon eggs and diamonds the size of walnuts, breezed, like jeweled butterflies, through the lobbies of the grand hotels. Rumors that Eva was engaged to the Prince von Hatzfeld-Wildenberg spread until Clara Huntington married him; then, there were rumors that she was engaged to Philippe de Bourbon. Finally, her mother announced she was engaged to the twenty-seven-year-old Prince Ferdinando Galatro-Colonna of Naples.

The wedding was held in the Papal Chapel in Paris. The floor was covered with violets and every seat not occupied by family was taken by society reporters.

Mrs. Mackay's dress "was simply perfect," one of the reporters gushed. It was "electric-blue, figured with shamrocks, and a small fortune in sapphires at the throat and wrists. The bonnet was blue, trimmed with an electric-blue aigrette" (a spray of egret feathers, such as horse guards wore on their helmets) "and golden-plumed hummingbirds. . . ."

Mr. Mackay, visibly less composed than Mrs. Mackay, sobbed loudly throughout the ceremony. When the wedding was over, the ever-vigilant press left the prince and princess to their honeymoon and rapturously followed Mrs. Mackay. "Mrs. Mackay is rumored to be going to London," they wrote, "to be presented to the queen in a dress that will cost a million dollars, the whole front to be of precious stones. . . ."

A storm of words followed her throughout Europe:

... At her Trouville cottage, the costliness of the table service and decorations reminds one of the Arabian Nights ... plates inlaid with cut gems ... flasks of amber ... flagons of gold....

... Mrs. Mackay has the largest and finest sapphire in the world and six parures of diamonds.... [*Parure*, which means a matched set, was one of the archaic words society writers adored.]

... All the ridiculous stories are pure inventions. Mrs. Mackay never wanted to illuminate the Arc de Triomphe, for instance, and never wanted to buy it....

Unfortunately, this story did not have a fairy-tale ending. Eight years later the princess left the prince and moved in with her mother in London. Still, once one becomes nobility, one must always belong to nobility. The princess saw to it that her daughter, with the very unlikely name Bianca Stigliano Colonna, was married to Count Jules de Bonvouloir.

The pursuit of exotic titles went on. The daughters of Ben Holladay, a crusty stagecoach driver who became the head of the Overland Stagecoach Company, went to Paris with their mother in search of husbands. When the proud Mrs. Holladay, who claimed she was descended from Mrs. Fitzherbert, the morganatic wife of King George IV of England, wired her husband that he was now the father-in-law of not only the Comte de Pourtales, but also the Baron de Boussiere, who were coming to visit him in San Francisco, Holladay packed his bags and fled to Oregon.

While the daughters of society were anxious to marry royalty, their sons sometimes preferred madams.

After their divorce, James Fair's wife was given custody of their two daughters, Tessie and Birdie; Fair was given the sons, James and Charles.

Mrs. Fair's two daughters were stunning social successes. Tessie married the highly respectable Hermann Oelrichs of New York, but Birdie married (nothing less than) a Vanderbilt, one William K. She entered the most sacred of sanctuaries, New York society.

James Fair was less successful with his sons. James, Jr., a young man muddled by alcoholism, died. His father, who still spent all his time in his office or drinking in Sausalito, hardly helped. The second son, Charles, was fully as independent and stubborn as his father. He set off on his own course.

On Wednesday, October 11, 1893, Charles, who had inherited some of his father's habits, went on a drinking binge in Sausalito. Before the day was over, he managed to fall off a bridge into a creek, and was dried off and locked in a hotel room. He escaped from the hotel room and was finally found wandering in the hills above the town, dressed only in an undershirt. He slept the entire next day. When he woke, he decided to elope.

James Fair and the rest of San Francisco were startled to read in the Friday papers that Fair, dressed in a blue traveling suit, appeared before a judge in Oakland on the arm of one Carrie Smith. The bride wore a blue jacket and sailor's hat with black feathers. Fair, who was twenty-six, gave his age as twenty-seven; Carrie Smith, who was thirty, dropped her age to twenty-six. The judge dutifully married them. A reporter who was present reported that Fair was perfectly steady and did not appear to have been drinking. Afterward, the couple celebrated by downing a quart of beer.

Almost everyone in San Francisco knew Carrie Smith as Maude Nelson, the Maude Nelson who ran what the newspapers tactfully called a "questionable resort" on Stockton Street. Certainly James Fair knew. When reporters pressed him for comment, he replied icily, "The boy is now nothing to me. I should not speak to him if I should meet him."

The San Francisco press corps was desperate to get in touch with Charles Fair and his new bride. No one in town liked his father, and everyone wanted to read about how his own son humiliated him. Charles Fair was just as anxious to get out of town to escape the explosion of publicity their elopement caused. He and Maude hopped on a train for New York.

When William Randolph Hearst, the editor of the *Examiner,* learned that Fair was about to escape, he was frantic. He telegraphed the sheriff in Port Costa (a town through which the train had to pass) commanding him to halt the train and take Fair off since he was clearly insane. Hearst signed the telegram, "Society for the Protection of Persons Charged with Insanity."

When the train arrived in Port Costa, the sheriff was waiting at the station, telegram in hand. A heated argument commenced. Railroad officials wanted their train to continue, and Fair wanted to know what the trouble was. In the meantime, a carriageload of *Examiner* reporters were riding at breakneck speed to Port Costa.

At last the railroad won the argument. The sheriff had no legal authority to hold the train and no one had ever heard of the "Society for the Protection of Persons

Charged with Insanity." The train pulled out of the station with Charles and Maude aboard, just as the carriageload of *Examiner* reporters reached the station. The *Examiner,* which never believed in letting the truth stand in the way of a good story, printed a screaming headline: ARRESTED AT PORT COSTA! FAIR IS CHARGED WITH INSANITY, BROUGHT BACK TO THIS CITY.

Charles and Maude arrived in New York, where they were thoroughly snubbed by his sisters. Then, they left for Europe where his father and the rest of the family hoped they would stay.

Within a year, he was back. The reason was the Fair fortune which he wanted to inherit; if he didn't get it, his sisters would. The only way to inherit it was to make up with his father. That seemed unlikely, but James Fair was very lonely, he was getting old, and Maude was a very charming woman. When James Fair died, on December 29, 1894, Charles Fair was the chief beneficiary of his will.

Charles now listed his occupation as "Capitalist." He began to indulge his taste for anything fast. At first it was racehorses, then it was speedboats, then racing cars.

In August 1902, he was driving a Mercedes Special along a road near Paris, with Maude on the seat beside him. He was driving very fast. As the car neared a small village, he realized he was trying to take a curve too quickly. He pushed on the brake and wrestled with the wheel, but it was too late; the car spun wildly, leaped off the side of the road, and cracked head-on into a tree. When the villagers hurried to the scene, they found the bodies of Charles and Maude near the wreckage. At the funeral, one of the hundreds of spectators outside the church stepped forward and plucked a flower from one of the floral displays. Within minutes the crowd, seeking souvenirs, tore all the displays to shreds.

The story of the people ends here, but great fortunes seem to have lives of their own. It was very important to the heirs to know whether Charles or Maude had been the first to die. If Maude died first, the Oelrichs and Vanderbilts in New York would get the money, since they were Charles' family; but, if Charles died first, Maude's relatives, who hurried to San Francisco from all over the United States, would get the fortune.

Each side engaged a battalion of lawyers, and the arguments went on at great length. Farmers were brought from the small French village to San Francisco, some to testify that they had seen a slight movement in Charles' foot, others claiming that they saw a tiny movement in Maude's hand. The case was finally settled out of court. Maude Fair's family was given a million dollars in return for their promise to drop the suit. Nevertheless, claimants for the fortune continued to appear as late as 1917, when Charles and Maude were almost forgotten.

Mary Hopkins tired of reporters continually poking into her private life and speculating about her fortune. She fled to her old home in Great Barrington, Massachusetts, and began constructing a new castle, this time of stone, at a cost of two million dollars. Evidently fascinated with building houses, she built a town house in New York, a summer home on Block Island and another house in Massachusetts. In 1886 she married Edward Searles, her interior decorator, who was twenty-two years younger than she.

Her adopted son Timothy, who was handling her business affairs in San Francisco, was understandably alarmed. He objected violently to the marriage. When Mary Hopkins died in 1891, she left her entire estate to Searles. Timothy sued and was finally given some eight million dollars, but Searles inherited the rest, which he used to travel and buy antiques. He donated the Nob Hill castle to the San Francisco Art Association.

Even William Sharon found himself pursued by reporters. In 1883 he was served with notice of divorce and demand for alimony. Sarah Althea Hill surfaced to claim that Sharon was secretly married to her, and she produced what she said was a marriage contract.

For the next several months, wars, politics and disasters were pushed off the front pages of the San Francisco newspapers. Acres of newsprint were devoted to the trial of William Sharon. Sharon's attorneys claimed that the contract was a forgery; Miss Hill's attorney, David Terry, the man who had shot Senator Broderick, called Sharon a "moral leper." The Chivalry was finally getting revenge on the Shovelry.

After several appeals, Sharon's lawyers were triumphant, but the exhausted Sharon died shortly afterward. Miss Hill married David Terry and saw him shot to death in a restaurant, in an argument over the case. She spent the rest of her life in a mental institution.

Meanwhile, Lillie Coit was not having a happy time. Her mother was absolutely determined to prove to her daughter that she should not have married Howard Coit. Mrs. Hitchcock found evidence that Coit had been something of a womanizer before he married Lillie. Gleefully she showed it to Lillie. Thereafter, whenever she could, Martha Hitchcock hinted to her daughter that her husband was unfaithful.

This was too much for Lillie. She had a nervous

breakdown. Finally, not knowing what to believe, she separated from Coit. She and Coit were both distressed. They wanted to find the words that would dispel the cloud of misunderstanding and bring them back together, but they were both proud. Lillie, goaded by her mother, could not trust her husband. Their letters bristled with defenses and accusations.

Coit died at the age of forty-seven in 1885. He left his entire fortune to Lillie. As she paged through his diary, she, to her surprise, found no evidence that he had ever cared for anyone else but her. Then, she realized what her mother had done.

From that day on, Lillie lived so recklessly that even San Franciscans were surprised. She washed her hair with champagne, dressed as a man to attend cockfights and played poker until the early hours of the morning. When some of her mother's friends came to call and she opened the door of her suite to them, they saw a boxing ring set up in the parlor and two professional boxers punching each other. If Mrs. Hitchcock was humiliated and outraged by her daughter's behavior, she kept it to herself. She died in 1899 at the age of eighty-one.

Unknown to Lillie, her mother had been paying a sum every year to a troublesome distant relative named Alexander Garnett. When the money stopped, Garnett came to Lillie. She had him thrown out. Garnett returned to Lillie's hotel suite a few days later. He had been drinking and had a gun. A friend of Lillie's, a former Confederate officer named Joseph McClung, opened the door. Garnett shot and killed him.

Hotel employees seized Garnett and he was tried and imprisoned. From prison, he announced that he would kill Lillie as soon as he was set free. Lillie was tired. She was sixty years old, and could see little point in staying in San Francisco under the threat of death—just to spite her mother. She packed her belongings and moved to Paris. San Francisco lost what the newspapers once called "its brightest ornament."

Society was relieved to see her go. Still yearning for the respectability of New York, they were ashamed of their recent riches, of how young their city was, of their colorful past. They wanted desperately to be established, to be *right*. Once charmed by Lillie Coit's mischievousness, they now found it only a painful reminder that they were not far removed from a mining camp. They were ashamed of Lillie Coit. When she left, one editor wrote, "Lillie Coit was once the idol of San Francisco. Now the city is too big and too old to have such idols."

Leland Stanford, the president of the Southern Pacific Railroad, former governor of California and United States senator, usually wore the smile of a man who had just heard a joke he didn't understand. Now, he was shaken by sobs, and tears ran down his cheeks. His son was dead.

Stanford had made great plans for the fifteen-year-old Leland, Jr. When the youngster showed an interest in archeology, Stanford brought in professors and explorers to talk with him and tutor him. He encouraged him to start his own collection of artifacts. He made arrangements for him to enter Harvard and bought a large town house in New York so both he and the boy's mother could be close to him. The Stanfords held an elaborate party for him in the ballroom of their mansion. To encourage his interests in archeology, the family went to Europe so the boy could see ruins and collect more artifacts. And there it had happened. The boy caught a fever and burned up and died. No one was able to do anything about it.

Stanford told his wife, "The children of California shall be our children." He made plans to build a university as a memorial to his son. It was a sentimental gesture, something Crocker, Hopkins or Huntington wouldn't have done. Hopkins would have been forgotten altogether had his name not been ressurected in 1926 for a hotel. Huntington and Crocker would be remembered for the library Huntington's nephew built in Southern California, and for the bank Crocker's son would found. Stanford's sentimental gesture won him the greatest fame of all. When he died in 1893, he was buried on the new campus of Leland Stanford Junior University in Palo Alto. Appropriately, his resting place was a very dignified granite mausoleum with two marble sphinxes on the steps.

The vice-president of the Society of California Pioneers sat on the back porch of his white frame house in Sonoma, watching his grapes ripen. Mariano Vallejo, who was now eighty-two, looked no older than fifty. He had looked fifty when he was twenty-five. His house was modest but comfortable. He had a cozy, dark library with a door that led to the front yard. He could reach out his bedroom window and pick an orange from the tree that overhung the roof or pick bunches of grapes from the arbor behind the house. Across the back lawn from where he sat was a tiny one-room house with a desk where he could work on his history of Spanish California and daydream. There were touches of Spain in the house: madonnas, simple dark furniture and old lace mantillas, but there was also a picture of Abraham Lincoln in the front hall to remind visitors that he was a citizen of the "happiest and freest nation of the world." He died peacefully on January 18, 1890, and was buried on a hillside not far from the house.

7. THE NOVELIST

Unknown to the Golden Circle, there was a spy in their ranks, a blond-haired, wide-eyed, sharp-tongued woman with a highly respected name who was writing novels about them. Her name was Gertrude Atherton.

Gertrude Atherton's grandfather was a gentle, romantic, and thoroughly impractical man, a distant cousin of Benjamin Franklin. He wandered west, launching and failing in one financial scheme after another as he crossed the country. He had more than enough vision and imagination, but lacked completely the cutthroat buccaneer spirit of a nineteenth-century capitalist. He let anyone and everyone take advantage of him. He brought Gertrude's mother with him, a woman Gertrude described as "beautiful, vivacious, flirtatious, fascinating, with a naturally brilliant mind and not an atom of common sense."

They came to San Francisco, where her grandfather

floundered pleasantly for a while making numerous friends and losing great quantities of money. William Ralston felt sorry for him and gave him a job as a secretary at the Bank of California. His charm, ancestry and his daughter's beauty and vivacity made them welcome in the parlors of the Chivalry. They were soon part of the social life of Rincon Hill. Gertrude's mother was kept busy receiving, entertaining and rejecting suitors by the dozen—a task she thoroughly enjoyed.

One man who came to call was not a southerner. An intense, strong-willed New Englander named Thomas Lodowick Horn, he was in the shipping business. He was so different from the easygoing, lighthearted southern young men she was used to that she was fascinated. The young men talked only of horseracing, the theater and who was going to Mrs. Parrott's latest ball, but Horn talked of himself and his plans. Finally, Horn proposed marriage. Gertrude's grandfather consulted William Ralston, and Ralston agreed that Horn's steadiness would be good for his rather airy daughter. They were married in a very formal ceremony with all of the Chivalry present.

It turned out to be the wedding of a rock and a hurricane. Gertrude's mother spent most of the time in hysterics; Horn spent his time either trying to argue her into line or, when that failed, ignoring her. Their civil war ended three years later, in 1860, with a divorce. Horn went his way with his shipping company; she went her way with a three-year-old daughter named Gertrude.

The Chivalry was willing to accept a marriage to a northerner, but they would not accept a divorce. Every door in South Park and Rincon Hill was closed. This was terrifying to Gertrude's mother; she needed the rare air and mannerisms of society.

When Gertrude was five, her mother sought readmission to society by marrying a young man named John Frederick Uhlorn. This, if possible, was a worse choice than Horn had been. Uhlorn came from (or rather, had been thrown out of) one of the most respected old Dutch families of New York. He had considerable charm but that was all. Most of his attention was given to gambling, which he enjoyed immensely, but was not very good at (which was why his family had thrown him out). Now he smiled broadly at his new wife and source of gambling money.

He did not smile broadly at Gertrude. Gertrude was now a pretty and precocious five-year-old, with her mother's high spirits and more than the sum of her mother's and father's headstrongness. She made a point of beating up other children who happened to be in the house and throwing them down the stairs—especially if her stepfather was present. She had a very fierce glare for a five-year-old.

When she saw what her husband was doing to her bank account, Gertrude's mother went into hysterics again. Her husband tried shouting at her, but that was ineffectual. Then he tried killing himself with chloroform, or perhaps, he let her think that was what he was trying to do to gain sympathy. That didn't work either. Finally Gertrude's grandfather caught him forging his wife's name on a check for a gambling debt. He handed Uhlorn a one-way ticket to South America which Uhlorn accepted.

By this time Gertrude had the manners of a wild

Apache. When her mother, who was looking for a new husband at the fashionable resort hotels, took her daughter along, Gertrude would behave with the decorum of a little princess until she reached the middle of the dining room. Then, with an ear-piercing screech, she would fling herself to the floor and beat it with her fists until her mother carried her away. To keep her still for her sewing lessons, her mother had to tie her to her chair. One day she threw the house into a panic by disappearing altogether. While her family searched frantically all over San Francisco, Gertrude was curled up in a laundry hamper reading *The Daughter of an Empress,* the spicy novel of the day.

Her grandfather decided it was time to civilize her. He summoned her into his dark-paneled library and told her that, from now on, she would read to him. That would keep her away from *The Daughter of an Empress.* Every day she was commanded to read to her grandfather.

At age seventeen, Gertrude, now a striking blond, was dispatched to the Sayre Institute in Kentucky, a private school for women. When she returned for the summer, prettier still, and no less headstrong, she discovered that her mother had a new suitor.

He was a dark-skinned, sleek, handsome young man named George Atherton. He was only twenty-four, fourteen years younger than Gertrude's mother. He was continually at the house. Gertrude observed he was "handsome and magnetic, he had fine manners, and he talked a great deal, although he never said anything." Her mother, who must have been flattered by Atherton's attentions, treated him kindly.

Then, Gertrude noticed, Atherton was looking at her. He began following her around the house when her

110

mother was gone. When they were alone, he proposed marriage. Gertrude laughed.

Atherton had the persistence of a spaniel. "I was sitting in the library one afternoon," Gertrude recalled, "reading the *Phaedo* of Plato.... I looked up with a scowl as he entered to propose for the sixth time.... I lowered my eyes ostentatiously to the book and turned my back. But he was not to be daunted. He talked and talked and talked. Finally, destiny answered for me, as I shrugged my shoulders saying, 'Oh well, I don't care. One has to marry sometime, I suppose. But do leave me in peace. I prefer Plato.'"

Atherton took her seriously. The next day as he was taking her on an errand in his carriage, he took a different turn in the road and took her directly to a church.

"For a moment I was dumbfounded," she said, "then furious, and threatened to jump out of the carriage. Then I began to feel dazzled. Surely this was romance and drama. I felt like the heroine of a novel."

She realized her mother would probably not feel nearly so dazzled. They decided to keep the marriage a secret until Atherton made arrangements with his family to move her to his house. Then she could tell her mother and grandfather and move out, avoiding the explosion she knew would follow.

She was sitting at dinner with her grandfather a week later, smiling inwardly, when her grandfather said: "I heard an amusing piece of gossip on the train today, that you and George Atherton were married. I suppose, as you are young and pretty, and he is young and handsome, rumors of this kind are inevitable."

"I felt as if a bomb had exploded," Gertrude recalled.

"I felt myself turning very red, but I looked him in the eye and said calmly, 'Well, it's true. We were married a week ago today and I'm going to town to meet him on Monday.'

"The twinkle vanished from his eyes. They looked like blue agates and his face turned white.... He merely, continued to stare at me for a moment, his lips set in a thin gray line. Then he left the table abruptly and went upstairs to my mother's room. He closed the door behind him and for two hours I heard the murmur of low voices."

He finally came back downstairs, where Gertrude waited. "I have little to say to you," he began. "You have been ungrateful to me and have acted disgracefully toward your mother. There was no reason for secrecy. No words can express my disappointment in you. As for that young man, whether he will make you happy or not remains to be seen. I do not think, however, that you will have any trouble with his family. They will be relieved that he has married a raw girl instead of a woman many years older than himself. They will no doubt receive you with open arms. You belong to them now. I am obliged to return to the city tomorrow afternoon. Kindly keep out of the way meanwhile. It will be some time before I shall wish to see you again."

She didn't see her mother or grandfather for three years. George picked her up on Monday and drove her to his family's estate south of San Francisco. It was an enormous area of land, beginning at the Bay and going nearly to the ocean on the other side of the Peninsula. It had once belonged to the Mexican governor Arguello, who called it "Las Pulgas," or "the Fleas" (which abounded there). The Athertons did not appreciate Ar-

guello's sense of humor. Now the plaque on the great
iron gate at the entrance to the estate read "Valparaiso
Park." George drove Gertrude through the gate and past
the ornamental hedges and trees on the lawn. It was a
full half-mile from the gate to the house.

George's father, a quiet New Englander named Faxon
Dean Atherton, and his mother, Dominga, a short and
very stout woman, were waiting for them on the front
porch.

Faxon Atherton traveled to San Francisco at the time
of the gold rush by way of Chile, where he stopped to
make a considerable fortune and to marry Dominga de
Goni, the daughter of a noble Spanish family in exile in
Valparaiso. They had lived on Rincon Hill when they
first arrived in San Francisco, but Dominga wanted the
hacienda life she remembered from Spain, so they moved
to the estate. They had since been joined by innumerable
relatives from Chile and Spain.

Faxon took George into the study to discuss his career and Gertrude was turned over to the unsmiling
Dominga—to be made into an Atherton.

The Athertons, as Gertrude soon learned, were to the
Peninsula what the Parrotts and Mrs. Eleanor Martin
were to San Francisco. They looked down on absolutely
everyone. Their position in society was fixed, unshakea-
ble and rooted back into the most unfathomable antiquity. They took great pride in how few people they felt
compelled to entertain. "I don't think I have ever met a
family so completely satisfied with themselves," Gertrude
wrote.

Since the Athertons looked on almost no one as their
social equal, their dinner guests were other Athertons or
de Gonis, most of the time. The cousins, second cousins

and third cousins would sit around the table eating eight- and ten-course dinners and gossiping noisily in Spanish. After supper, the men would move to the parlor to talk business and smoke cigars; the women went to the sitting room to embroider and gossip. Since Dominga Atherton's English vocabulary was limited to a few words and Gertrude spoke no Spanish, Gertrude was not a lively participant. "I merely sat among them," she said, "stifling yawns and listening vaguely."

Gertrude began excusing herself after supper and fleeing to her room. Ever since her grandfather had forced her to read the classics, Gertrude felt a desire to exact revenge from English literature. Now, alone in her room, she began to compose short, gossipy stories about Peninsula society. She sent some of them to the *Argonaut,* a San Francisco magazine, under a fanciful pen name. To her surprise, they were printed.

Encouraged, she put together all the gossip, scandal, malicious stories, untruths, half-truths, slanders, libels, rumors and exaggerations she had ever heard into one gorgeous story, which she called *The Randolphs of Redwoods.*

The novel told the tale of a wealthy society woman who dragged her innocent daughter down into a life of shame and degradation by handing her bottles of gin at unfortunate moments. Its style combined the seriousness of purpose of *The Daughter of an Empress* with the lightness and humor of Hume's *History of England.* What made it fascinating was the characters she put in it. Everyone in San Francisco society from Judge McAllister to Mrs. Parrott to the Athertons, though thinly disguised, was recognizable. The *Argonaut* bought

114

The Randolphs of Redwoods for $150 and began running it anonymously by chapter.

When the first chapter appeared, San Francisco society turned red. Those who recognized themselves exploded with rage; those who couldn't find themselves were angry they had been left out. Everyone was upset by some part of the story. It was obvious that the story was written by someone inside society, so attention turned to exposing the perpetrator of this outrage. Suspected authors were snubbed on the street or had their names crossed off invitation lists.

No one, of course, suspected Gertrude Atherton. While everyone in the sitting room of the Atherton house talked excitedly about the story, repeating the juicier episodes, guessing who was who and arguing about who the author was, Gertrude sat smiling and quietly knitting. No one asked her opinion.

8. EARTHQUAKE AND AFTERSHOCK

In the darkness of the empty Opera House that James Flood and John Mackay built, the crystal prisms of the great chandelier (the largest in the world) began to tremble. It was five fifteen on the morning of April 18, 1906.

The floor of the Opera House was strewn with paper programs. Hours earlier, the Opera House had been shaking with applause and the crystal prisms had reflected the gorgeous costumes of the Metropolitan Opera Company. Enrico Caruso bowed. Row after row of men and women in dark evening dress and elaborate gowns with circles of diamonds flashing stood and applauded. Gradually the applause faded, the curtain closed and the audience filed out noisily.

The chandelier shuddered. The tinkling of the glass prisms was joined by the creaking of wooden walls and the dry crackle of splitting plaster. The brass gong in the orchestra pit rang softly by itself.

The wood creaking became a screech. A sound like fingernails on a chalkboard made by thousands of bricks twisting and rubbing against each other began to be heard. There was an abrupt ripping sound. The great chandelier broke free, whistled down and smashed the seats with a tremendous crash.

Phyllis de Young, age thirteen, woke in her family's huge Victorian house on California Street. A large picture of the Madonna swung out and hit the ceiling, then swung back and hit the wall over her head.

Kate Peterson, also thirteen, who would soon marry John Ward Mailliard, Jr., the grandson of Adolph Mailliard, the illegitimate grandson of a Bonaparte, was also awakened by the earthquake. She sat up, saw what was happening, and promptly went back to sleep.

In her room at the Berkeley Inn, Gertrude Atherton leaped from her bed and opened the door so it would not be sprung from its hinges, trapping her inside. She had been through earthquakes before. "The earth danced, and leaped, and plunged, and roared," she recalled. "This is the end of California, I thought. We are going to the bottom of the Pacific. . . ." Fifty-five seconds later, it stopped. A silence greater than the sound of the earthquake followed; then it was broken by the sound of voices and doors opening.

San Francisco society, dressed in their robes, stood in front of their houses amid the rubble of fallen chimneys and broken ornament. It hadn't seemed that bad. Those on Nob Hill looked to the southeast, toward Rincon Hill. A pall of dirty, yellow-brown smoke, glowing in the early morning light, was rising from the hill. Under it, they could see orange flames flickering.

Most of the brick and cement office buildings downtown survived the earthquake intact. As he walked through the hallways with his staff, the manager of the Palace Hotel found only a few small cracks in the walls and a great deal of broken plaster on the carpet. He hurried back to the lobby to reassure the guests.

South of Market Street, near Rincon Hill, it was a different matter. The rows of rooming houses there were built on loose-filled land over the Bay. When the earthquake hit, the earth sagged six feet, the wooden boarding-houses collapsed like card houses, dropping hot stoves and cooking breakfasts onto the piles of kindling. Fifty-seven fires started at once.

On Steuart Street, the firemen of Engine Company 58 hooked their hose onto a hydrant and opened the valve. A thin stream of muddy water dribbled out. The water mains had snapped like twigs when the earth moved.

From Nob Hill, the residents could see a stream of refugees moving slowly west and north. They moved away from the fire, pushing carts and wheelbarrows and dragging trunks filled with their belongings; a few were even pushing bulky upright pianos. The great pall of smoke hung over all of Market Street. They could hear the distant popping and cracking of falling wood and bursting metal.

All the guests, including Enrico Caruso and the Metropolitan Opera Company, fled the Palace Hotel. Harry Tevis picked up half a dozen singers in his new automobile and drove them to the safety of Golden Gate Park. The smell of fire was very strong. They could hear the roar of wind being sucked into the flames only ten blocks away.

Michael de Young watched the fire from his bedroom window. The servants had already taken the horses and

119

the two cows to safety in Golden Gate Park. His daughters, each carrying a pet dog, were getting ready to walk to the Ferry Building for the trip across the Bay to their house in San Rafael. "Well," de Young said, "I'm standing here watching everything I own burn."

Charles Frederick Crocker filled a tugboat with sacks and boxes of money from the Crocker Bank. When the tugboat was loaded, it chugged out into the Bay to wait for the end of the fire.

Rancher Henry Miller, who was now seventy-nine, left his South Park house to see if his business survived. Cavalrymen blocked his way downtown. When he returned to his house, the fire was approaching. He helped his crippled son, Henry, Jr., into a wagon and drove south to safety.

On Nob Hill, the residents and hundreds of refugees and curious from the western part of the city watched the fire on Market Street. They could see the flag of the Palace Hotel and streams of water dancing on its roof against the brown curtain of smoke. The fire moved methodically from building to building down Market Street. The Wells Fargo Building burned, then the Grand Hotel, then sparks showered the roof of the Palace. The manager and staff fled before the windows in the upper stories of the hotel shattered from the heat and the draperies exploded in flames.

Several ash- and oil-covered, black automobiles appeared in front of the unfinished Fairmont Hotel on Nob Hill. Out of them stepped a grim-faced Mayor Eugene Schmitz, the chief of police, and the newly-appointed members of the Committee for Safety. Their headquarters had been at Portsmouth Square near the Embarcadero, but that was now directly in the path of the fire.

The men filed into the ballroom of the Fairmont and sat on the unpacked crates of furnishings. A few minutes later an automobile driven by a soldier stopped in front of the Fairmont. General Frederick Funston, carrying maps of San Francisco under his arm, climbed out and strode into the hotel. A few minutes later, he was describing his plan to dynamite all the buildings along Van Ness Avenue in the center of the city, in order to create a great firebreak.

The Crocker butler carefully wrapped Millet's "Man with a Hoe," which Ethel Crocker, who had a premonition of disaster before she and her husband left for Europe, ordered him to save before anything else. The frightened butler rescued the Millet, but left the rest of the Crocker collection to the flames. In the old Stanford mansion (which, since the death of Mrs. Stanford, housed the city offices of Stanford University) the staff was carrying out crates filled with the knickknacks and memorabilia Governor Stanford had collected. In the Hopkins mansion, now the San Francisco Institute of Art, Alma deBretteville and dozens of other students were frantically carrying paintings and pieces of sculpture out the great Gothic doorway.

When the Committee for Safety got back in their automobiles and drove to the west and safe side of Van Ness Avenue, Nob Hill was deserted. It was getting dark.

"I spent that night watching the hills of San Francisco burn," Gertrude Atherton wrote. "Columns of flames that looked to be miles high, rolling, twisting, gyrating masses of smoke shot with a billion sparks."

In the early hours of the morning, the mansions of Nob Hill became huge bonfires. The Tevis, Tobin and Haggin houses, with their libraries and great stables and

observation towers, blazed. The Crockers' Moorish palace–railroad depot collapsed. The Georgian-porticoed
Huntington house, the white-packing-crate Stanford
mansion, with its marble zodiac, and finally Mary
Hopkins' fantastic Gothic castle blazed fiercely and then
collapsed in great cascades of flame.

The fire burned for two more days before it was
stopped at Van Ness Avenue. General Funston's dyna-
miting successfully contained it and the last isolated fires
were extinguished.

The former residents and the curious came to sift
through the four hundred and ninety square blocks of
ruins, picking their way through the still-smoking wreckage. Private guards watched ruined bank buildings,
whose steel vaults were still too hot to open. Khaki-
uniformed soldiers patrolled the ruins for looters.

Rincon Hill was an eerie forest of charred timbers and
chimneys. South Park stood like a ruined fortress. Its
fire-gutted brick houses, their iron balconies twisted by
heat, were a solitary island in a black lake of collapsed
wooden buildings. Nob Hill was littered with dead cats
and soot-blackened statues left behind by art students.
Only the brownstone Flood mansion and the unfinished
Fairmont Hotel still stood.

On Van Ness Avenue, Rudolph Spreckels looked im-
passively at the burnt mahogany, twisted, gold-plated
faucets, fragments of Algerian marble and chips of fres-
coed ceilings where his house stood before it was blown
to bits by dynamite.

Workmen, sorting through the rubble of the Opera
House, found an enormous blackened glob of melted
crystal and brass, once the largest chandelier in the
world.

Two weeks after the fire was put out, the thirty feet of rubble that clogged Market Street was gone. The first streetcar rumbled along the street, cheered by the men working in the ruins on either side. Mayor Schmitz, grinning broadly, ran the streetcar. Behind him, leaning from the windows of the flag-decked car and waving at the onlookers, Patrick Calhoun, the president of the streetcar company, the county supervisors, and Abraham Ruef, the political leader of San Francisco, were passengers.

Not everyone was cheering the mayor and the city government. A few blocks from Market Street, in a small shack that was serving as the temporary headquarters of the First National Bank, the president of that bank, Rudolph Spreckels, was sitting with the nation's most famous prosecutor, Francis J. Heney, and the nation's most famous detective, William J. Burns. They were planning to pull down the government of San Francisco. San Francisco's government was the most corrupt in the United States. In a truly San Franciscan fashion, it was not just corrupt, but flamboyantly, wildly, extravagantly, almost hilariously corrupt.

San Francisco's government was a practical joke played on the citizenry by a small, balding man with a handlebar mustache and bright, twinkling eyes, named Abraham Ruef. Ruef had an agile mind. At age fourteen, he went to the University of California and graduated at eighteen with a degree in classical languages. He organized the student cooperative there, was successful in student politics and wrote a thesis on "Purity in Politics" that won acclaim from the faculty. He then went to Hastings Law School; when he was twenty-one, he had his law degree.

123

He went into private practice in San Francisco. On the strength of his mind and his great energy, he might well have become another Hall McAllister, a great attorney, then judge, and a leader of society—except that he was a Jew. San Francisco was willing to accept him. Jews were more acceptable in this city than in the rest of the United States at the turn of the century, that is, they were accepted as brilliant artists or financiers or lawyers, but not as people. Ruef would not be welcome in society, his children would never go to a Greenway Cotillion, he would not be asked to join any of the businessmen's clubs, and he would never receive an invitation to dine with Mrs. Eleanor Martin. Ruef took this with great tolerance and humor. If San Francisco society would not accept him, then he would make fools of them.

In 1901, Ruef had organized his own party, the Union Labor Party and began putting together a government. As his candidate for mayor, Ruef chose Eugene Schmitz, the president of the Musician's Union, a tall, extremely handsome man with wavy black hair and an elegant black beard. He was an excellent violinist, a good conductor of theater orchestras, and a composer of some interesting, if not exactly brilliant, marches. He knew almost nothing about politics; that was Ruef's domain. To the astonishment of almost everyone, Schmitz defeated both the Republican and Democratic candidates.

The newspapers and much of San Francisco now settled back to watch the battle begin. Schmitz, the first and only labor mayor in the United States, was certain to be locked in struggle with the city's great capitalists within days of his election. To their astonishment, he wasn't. There were nothing but smiles between Schmitz and the city's business leaders. There was an even more

124

astonishing announcement: the papers noted that Schmitz had been invited to dinner by Mrs. Eleanor Martin. Elegantly dressed, Schmitz smiled at reporters as he stepped from his carriage and walked up the steps of the impressive mansion and greeted the venerable Mrs. Martin.

Mayor Schmitz began building an ornate mansion at the corner of Vallejo and Pierce streets. The mansion cost thirty thousand dollars, a remarkable sum, because the mayor's salary was only six thousand dollars a year. When the house was completed, Schmitz showed visitors through it. In the salon was a twelve-hundred-fifty-dollar Persian carpet, a gift from the financier J. Downey Harvey, the son of Mrs. Eleanor Martin.

There was so little animosity between Schmitz's administration and the city's businessmen that a businessman found he could do almost anything he desired, if he had a good attorney, such as Abraham Ruef.

If there was a male equivalent to Mrs. Eleanor Martin, it was Patrick Calhoun. With a stern face and a drooping white mustache, Calhoun looked like an Austrian archduke; his manner led one to believe he shared the illusion. He was the president of the United Railroads, San Francisco's privately owned streetcar system, the grandson of Senator John C. Calhoun, and the son of Andrew Pickens Calhoun, the second-wealthiest cotton planter in the South. When the Civil War wiped his family out, he became the personal agent of J. Pierpont Morgan, founded the Southern Railroad, and came to San Francisco to take over the many small streetcar and cable car companies there and merge them into one tremendous company. His self-confidence was as remarkable as his rage against anyone who blocked his way.

Even the *Chronicle,* an extravagant admirer of his, found him often "exhibiting corporate arrogance in its most exasperating form." His manners were perfect, and, if anyone considered him arrogant, he shrugged his shoulders. He was the very quintessence of Chivalry, the last standing pillar of Southern society, and one of the most powerful men in San Francisco.

Calhoun strode into the office of the counsel of the United Railways, the former attorney general of California, Tirey L. Ford. A man with a handlebar mustache and twinkling eyes was with him.

"This is Mr. Ruef," Ford said. "One of our prominent attorneys and influential men, who is our good friend and can be of service to us."

Since Schmitz had been elected mayor, Ruef had been receiving five hundred dollars a month from the United Railways. "Everyone has heard of Mr. Ruef," Calhoun said, shaking his hand. "I am glad to know him and hope to know him better." Shortly thereafter, Ruef's fee increased to one thousand dollars a month.

The newspapers were not long in discovering what was going on. "If you wish a job for yourself or your friend," the *Chronicle* wrote, "you must see Ruef. If you wish a license for a grog-shop or theater, you must see Ruef. If you desire to construct a building in defiance of the fire ordinances, you must see Ruef. . . . Ruef is by all odds the most dangerous boss this city has hitherto endured."

Without ever going to court or visiting a client, Ruef had the most thriving legal practice in town. He represented the most prestigious companies: the Pacific States Telephone and Telegraph Company, the Pacific Gas and Electric Company, and a dozen others. He was also the attorney for the leading figures in San Francisco society. Among them was Patrick Calhoun of the United Railroads and William Tevis, who inherited the great Nob Hill house (destroyed in the fire) with its huge library from his father, and who now, through his Bay Cities Water Company, wanted to sell some of his watershed land around Lake Tahoe to the city. (Tevis tried to sell the water rights for two hundred thousand dollars and failed; he hired Ruef, who raised the price to ten million dollars, one million of which he would get. The city was on the verge of buying it.) He was the attorney for the socially prominent Frank Drum, the leading stockholder and director of the Pacific Gas and Electric Company. He received only five hundred dollars a month for this service. He was the attorney for William Crocker, son of Charles Crocker and the owner of the Crocker-Woolworth Bank and the Parkside Realty Company. Yet he rarely met these men; in practice, he dealt almost entirely through their assistants. Later these prominent men would claim they did not know their assistants were bribing Ruef.

Rudolph was the youngest son of Claus Spreckels, the man who won the island from the king of Hawaii in a poker game and went on to build a great sugar empire. The young Rudolph fought and argued with his father from the time he was a teenager. He even set aside his allowance and invested it until he was a multimillionaire on his own at age twenty-six. His businesses competed with his father's. This so annoyed the old man that he tried to keep all the banks on the West Coast from granting credit to Rudolph. Despite this, he had a great admiration for his son. When his son's gas company stole a franchise from his gas company, he proudly told his friends, "I was never beaten but once in my life, and by my own boy, too!"

Rudolph, who was now thirty-four, had a square face,

a trim mustache, and unsmiling blue eyes. He walked very stiffly and had the manners of a Prussian count. He rarely talked about anything except business, and told friends (with some pride) that he had never voted in an election. For diversion, Rudolph kept a large estate in Burlingame where he could spend his free time talking about business to anyone with whom he had not talked business in San Francisco. His humorlessness and dedication were matched only by his absolutely scrupulous honesty. Even the slightest dishonesty made him cold with rage.

The streetcar running down Market Street with Schmitz, Calhoun and Ruef aboard set off Rudolph Spreckels' anger. Before the earthquake, the United Railways sought permission to run its streetcars under overhead electric wires. These wires were cheap to hang, but they were ugly. Spreckels preferred underground electric conduits. In fact, he thought that the city, and not a private company, should run the streetcars. He and former mayor James Phelan offered to build a municipal railway for the city, and sell it back to them at cost. Mayor Schmitz said he would consider the idea.

One month after the earthquake, the Board of Supervisors, under the direction of Abraham Ruef, granted a franchise to run streetcars from overhead wires to United Railways, whose assistant counsel was also Abraham Ruef.

Spreckels and Phelan, knowing that the Schmitz administration would be reluctant to prosecute itself, agreed to finance an investigation themselves. Burns would do the investigating, and Heney would bring charges and take the men to court. Spreckels insisted on only one thing; that Heney not stop at Ruef. He wanted

Red-bearded Charles Crocker (above), who, like his fellow multimillionaires, built a monstrous home on Nob Hill.

Dashing Lillie Hitchcock Coit found tragedy in the one great love of her life.

Mark Hopkins (right), who did not share his partners' enthusiasm for conspicuous consumption.

The Society of California Pioneers

Governor Leland Stanford (right), thrived on the glory due a railroad president.

Mrs. Leland Stanford shared her husband's interest in the university they founded as a memorial to their only son.

As an infant, Leland Stanford, Jr. (below) was presented to his parents' friends at a dinner party on a flower-garlanded silver tray.

The Society of California Pioneers

James Flood, who went from proprietor of the Auction Lunch to King of the Comstock Lode.

The St. Francis Hotel, built by the Crocker family, then rebuilt after the 1906 earthquake and fire.

A production at Bohemian Grove.

The "Cremation of Care" ceremony at the Grove.

. M. Molotov of the Soviet
elegation to the United Na-
ons charter conference.

Ir. and Mrs. James Flood,
osts at their Woodside
ome to Anthony Eden dur-
g the U.N. conference.

Harold L. Mack, Jr.

Harold L. Mack, Jr.

Ernest Hemingway and Ingrid Bergman

Mrs. William Wallace (Ina Claire), Sir Charles Mendl and Mrs. Robert Hayes Smith

MONDAY LUNCH
AT THE ST. FRANCIS

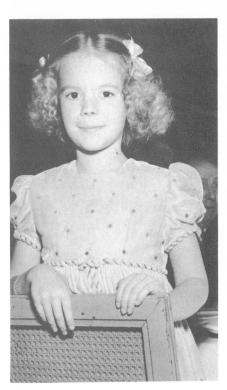

Natalie Wood

Desi Arnaz and Lucille Ball

Kathleen Norris

Society editors lead the grand march at a Mardi Gras in the 1950s: Frances Moffat (*Examiner*), Marie Hicks Davidson (*Call-Bulletin*), Mildred Brown Robbins (*Chronicle*).

The Garden Court of the Palace Hotel during the 1959 Cotillion.

An Olympic Ball (above) at the St. Francis honoring members of the International Olympic Committee. Comte de Beaumont of the IOC is seen here with Mrs. Thomas Wertheimer.

One of the daily luncheons (above right) at Squaw Valley during the Olympics. Mrs. Robert Ducas (then Georgiana de Ropp Meyer) kisses Avery Brundage, head of the IOC, as Mrs. Richard Walker, organizer of the luncheons, looks on.

Squaw Valley, 1960: Billy Pearson, the jockey who became an art dealer, and Mrs. William (Buster) Collier, wife of the screen star, ham it up.

Edward Carroll

Celia Cebrian, whose early death was one of the Jet Set's tragedies, liked to dabble in witchcraft and celebrated her birthday on Halloween.

Another glamorous Mrs. Jose Cebrian, Gretchen Kirsch. She left him in a friendly divorce after the couple had had two children.

Gail Sokolow

**Mrs. Thomas Carr Howe and Mrs. John Gallois
at the California Palace of the Legion of Honor.**

Crowds outside the Opera House ogle Phyllis Fraser, Queen of the Jet Set.

Phyllis Fraser does the Twist following an early '60s Opera opening.

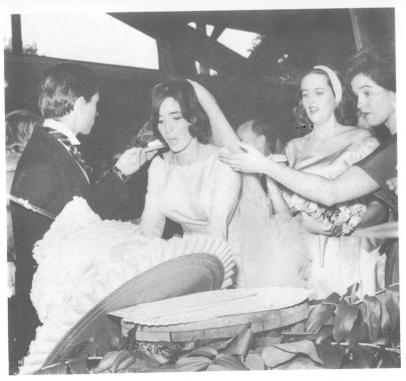

At the wedding of Natalie Owings, daughter of the famous architect, and John Fell Stevenson, son of Adlai: there was great excitement when the bride cut the cake and it nearly fell off the table.

Post-Cotillion deb Elizabeth Cooper was married on horseback to Jesse Brown, a policeman, at a ranch near Fresno. It was a period in the late '60s and early '70s when the young were getting married on mountaintops

Elsie Metcalf, a fifth-generation Huntington, was escorted to the 1970 Cotillion by Stephen Brown, who later became a disciple and teacher of the Maharishi Mahesh Yogi.

Dressed to attract attention at the 1976 Opera opening, party girl Joan Hitchcock, last of the Jet Set, arrives with Milton Harper, "Mr. Nightlife."

Energetic Mrs. John Ward Mailliard III (above) at one of the many charity parties she organizes for society, this one at the Palace of Fine Arts.

Shirley Temple Black (above right).

Mrs. Bing Crosby and John Scott Trotter.

Mr. and Mrs. Christian de Guigne III.

Mr. and Mrs. Richard Cooley.

the investigation to go all the way into the parlors on Nob Hill and the back rooms of the businessmen's clubs. On November 15, Ruef and Mayor Schmitz were indicted for extortion.

In the business clubs and on Nob Hill, Spreckels and Heney were the heroes of the hour. When they lunched at the University Club or the Pacific Union Club, prominent men of San Francisco stopped by their table to congratulate them and inquire about the prosecution.

Ruef was locked in a hotel room at the Little St. Francis (a temporary wooden structure in Union Square used while the earthquake damage to the St. Francis itself was repaired). He didn't seem glum about his prospects. "I feel as jolly as a clam at high tide," he told the reporters who came to see him. He was not exactly suffering in his life as a convict; his luncheon menu that day (paid for by the city) featured oysters, Russian caviar, planked smelts, fried sweetbreads, squab, lobster salad, cocktails and French wine.

But Burns was very thorough. He wanted proof that the supervisors were willing to accept bribes, so he instructed one of his agents to approach supervisor Lonergan and offer him five hundred dollars if he would get a city ordinance passed. Lonergan was invited to the agent's house. Burns and two witnesses hid behind a double door. While Burns listened, the agent explained what he wanted and offered Lonergan the money. Lonergan took it.

Burns stepped from behind the door. When Lonergan saw the detective, he turned to the agent and shouted, "I want you to arrest this man! He bribed a supervisor!"

Burns smiled. "Yes, I saw him do it."

With the help of Lonergan's testimony, Heney was able

to win seventy-five new indictments for bribery and extortion against Ruef, Mayor Schmitz, the chief of police and the entire San Francisco board of supervisors. Then, to the shock of San Francisco society, he pressed beyond that. Indictments were handed down against Louis Glass, the vice-president of Pacific Telephone, Frank Drum, the director of the gas company, J.E. Green, the president of the Parkside Realty Company, Tirey Ford, the counsel of the United Railroads, and Patrick Calhoun, the president of the United Railroads. William Crocker offered to stand bail for Calhoun.

Suddenly Spreckels and Heney found they were unpopular in the business clubs and on Nob Hill. No one stopped by their table anymore. They were considered traitors to their class.

A wealthy woman visiting from the East complained, "You dare not express any opinion for fear your companion may be under indictment; or if he should not be, you are sure his brother or best friend is, or his sister is engaged to one who is."

Gertrude Atherton recalled, "Old friends ceased to speak, sisters cut each other, people entertaining were given to understand that one party or the other must be invited at a time, and one dame went so far as to demand the sympathies of her guests as they entered her drawing room; if they declared for the prosecution, they were requested to leave."

The newspapers turned against the prosecution. The *Examiner* referred to Spreckels as the "Emperor Rudolph." The *Argonaut* said, "No man has the right to buy himself a position of moral authority." Spreckels' motives were questioned; he was accused of wanting to be mayor or wanting the United Railroads franchise for himself.

Angered by the criticism, Spreckels replied, "I do not want to be mayor. I do not want the franchise of the United Railroads. The peculiar position in which I have been placed is distasteful to me. Do you suppose I enjoy prosecuting and bringing disgrace and public odium upon men who have been associated with me in business, and perhaps men who have been my dearest and best friends?

"In instituting this graft investigation, I was actuated by a broader motive than the mere punishment of wrongdoers and the moral cleaning up of a city. Any man who thinks can see that this country is in danger of a revolution. Our menace is the growth of bitter class feeling. Poor men are coming to believe that very rich men may break the law when and where they choose. Some rich men, I am sorry to say, are coming to believe so too.

"My greatest purpose in using my resources as a private citizen and bringing these rich corporations and rich bribe-grivers to justice is to try to do something toward healing this terrible and growing breach between the classes. . . . I went into this resolved to let justice hit whoever was found guilty, be it my friend, my business associate, my enemy, or myself."

The board of supervisors resigned. Grants of immunity were urged by Heney to those who testified against Calhoun and the others. Mayor Schmitz was the first to be convicted. He was sentenced to five years in prison. Then, one by one, the trials of San Francisco's business leaders began.

Supervisor James L. Gallagher was the principal witness to Ruef's bribery of the supervisors. On April 21, a bomb blew out the front of the house where he was staying. A short while later, Gallagher was scheduled to visit some rental flats he was repairing. At the moment he was to have arrived, dynamite blew the flats to pieces. Gallagher was still at his downtown office and missed the explosions.

On November 13, Francis Heney was at the prosecution table in the courtroom during a trial recess joking with a clerk from the district attorney's office. A man in an overcoat walked up to him, quickly pulled a revolver from his pocket, aimed and shot him in the throat.

Heney, remarkably, survived the wound. The man who shot him claimed he acted on his own to settle a personal grudge against Heney. The matter was never settled in court, because the assailant was found dead in his jail cell the next day, a bullet hole in his forehead. There was a pistol nearby, and the police insisted it was suicide.

Two weeks later the police chief of San Francisco, William Biggy, under fire from the press for letting the man die, either fell or jumped into the San Francisco Bay from a police launch. He was drowned. At the same time, the cashbooks of the United Railways, recording all the financial transactions of the company for the period in question, disappeared mysteriously.

As each of the dozen defense attorneys filed motions to delay the trials, the prosecution's case sagged. Key witnesses disappeared. The prosecution faced a city and a press with a very short attention span. They were tired of the trials and eager to move on to something else.

But Heney was stubborn. He pressed on with the prosecution of Calhoun. Calhoun's attorney, A.A. Moore, again attacked Spreckels' motives.

"It isn't in human nature," Moore argued, "that Heney and Spreckels should have done these things without a motive. I cannot imagine myself doing it.... No man lives who would have given up his money and his time merely for the love of his country!"

Heney, red with anger, replied: "Mr. Moore has told you that he cannot imagine Mr. Spreckels or myself acting in this manner without a motive. Moore will probably tell you that George Washington went through Valley Forge because he wanted to be known as 'The Father of his Country,' and that Abraham Lincoln was a hoax, merely another Spreckels seeking to acquire some property that didn't belong to him.... While we were turning out the boodling supervisors and sending a corrupt mayor to prison, these men were sending notes of warning to Ruef, and now they have the audacity to come here and tell you that we must have been actuated by false motives. My God! Is that the sort of thing that is to receive the approval of San Francisco?"

As a matter of fact, it was. Louis Glass of the Pacific Telephone Company was found guilty, but his conviction was overturned by the State Supreme Court. The opinion freeing Glass was written by Justice Frederick Henshaw, who himself was later convicted of taking a four-hundred-ten-thousand-dollar bribe from the heirs of James Fair to break his will. Frank Drum's indictment was thrown out because the chief witness against him, James Gallagher, disappeared. After the indictment was thrown out, Gallagher reappeared.

The charges against J.E. Green, the president of the Parkside Realty Company, were dropped when he agreed to testify against Ruef. Mayor Eugene Schmitz's conviction was overturned by the State Supreme Court, because, among other reasons, the indictment against him named him "Eugene Schmitz," not "Mayor Eugene Schmitz." After three trials, Patrick Calhoun and his assistant, Tirey L. Ford, were found not guilty.

In the end, only Abraham Ruef was found guilty. He was convicted of accepting a two-hundred-thousand-dollar bribe from Patrick Calhoun and his assistant, Tirey Ford, to arrange the trolley franchise.

Heney wanted to continue the trials. With the support of Rudolph Spreckels, he ran for district attorney in the 1909 election. San Francisco was tired of graft trials, and tired of Francis J. Heney's enthusiasm. He was defeated by a candidate from the Union Labor Party, who pledged there would be no more trials. Heney, too, learned the lesson that everyone loves a reformer as long as he doesn't actually reform anything. Disgusted, Rudolph Spreckels returned to his business.

On March 7, 1911, Abraham Ruef was taken to San Quentin prison to serve a sentence of four years and seven months. Ruef kept silent throughout the trial. His word would have convicted Calhoun, Ford, Glass, Drum or Green, but he refused to speak. At San Quentin he remained good humored. He wrote a Fourth of July skit for the prisoners in which they played the roles of San Francisco's society leaders.

9. MASQUERADE

Along the Barbary Coast, the underworld whirled in fantastic steps to the rhythmic tunes of banging pianos, banjos, tom-toms and blaring brass horns ... from Barbary Coast dives to the Hotel St. Francis came the Banjo with Herman Heller as orchestra leader, soon to be followed by Art Hickman's introduction of the saxophone which would bring the jazz to the modern era.

> Ragtime and Jazz, pre-World War I, from *San Francisco,* American Guide Series, 1947.

With the headlines full of sordid accounts of bribery, extortion, labor troubles and bombings and the industrial expansion in and around San Francisco turning the peaceful hills south of Market Street into grimy expanses of factory, railroad yard and warehouse, it was natural for San Francisco society to yearn for quieter, more pleasant times and places.

The San Francisco that rose from the rubble of the 1906 fire bore little resemblance to the ornamental wooden city that stood before it. The fantastic wooden castles on Nob Hill were gone, replaced by solid brick and concrete hotels and apartment houses. The fantastic Palace Hotel with its grand court and bay windows was gone. It was replaced by a new Palace Hotel, a brick structure that looked exactly like the office buildings on either side of it. Downtown San Francisco no longer looked like a colorful mixture of Constantinople, Paris and Coney Island. The spires and domes and gingerbread were replaced by square banks and office blocks that might have been moved in from Chicago or Cincinnati. The business leaders took great pride in the transformation; their idea of sublime architecture was a Roman-porticoed bank, not a romantically fashioned interpretation of a cuckoo clock or a Parisian bordello. They were proud that their city now looked respectable.

But there was something sad about the change. Lillie Hitchcock Coit came back to the city in 1919 and told Gertrude Atherton, "It is no longer a wild place. Like me, it has settled down." Even the saloons, dives and dance halls of the Barbary Coast (which San Francisco had tolerated with pride because they enhanced the city's image as "The Paris of the West") were blockaded and closed down by the police.

This much industry and respectability was fine for the Chamber of Commerce, but it also made the city just a little boring. Fantasy was the best way to counter boredom.

The Golden Circle had the money to make any fantasy real. Thanks to the recent invention of the automobile, they could move outside the city like knights errant.

The first automobile was brought to San Francisco by young Charlie Fair in 1893. A Panhard, made in France, it looked like an oversized wheelchair and sounded like a badly strained coffee percolator when it was running properly. When it wasn't running properly (which was most of the time), it sounded like a gasworks blowing up. Before it had been in San Francisco a month, it made mortal and lifelong enemies of every horse and pedestrian in the city. It also had made Charlie the envy of every man and boy in town.

Less than twenty years later, everyone in society had an automobile. Cars pushed carriages out of coach houses and were treated like precocious children by their owners. Handcrafted in England, France or Italy or by family-run firms in the East, they were more land-yachts than transportation. Their interiors were furnished in leather, brass and mahogany like small country houses. Their engines were as complex and had as many parts as Swiss watches. Unfortunately, they did not run quite as well as Swiss watches. The larger the engine, the slower the car. Whenever one of these machines succeeded in making the long drive from San Francisco to Los Angeles, the event was reported in the newspapers. Their wealthy owners insisted on trying to drive everywhere: through streams, across deserts, and even up the abominable wagon roads to Yosemite Valley.

In 1910 the Sunday morning stillness of the farms and eucalyptus groves south of San Francisco were shattered by a terrible noise. An awful rattling and coughing sent terrified squirrels running for trees and drove the birds to flight. Several minutes later the source of the noise came into view: it was an enormous steel, wood and glass automobile, decorated with a colorful spray of American flags on the nose of its long hood. The outside of the car was hung with spare tires, tool boxes, gasoline cans, wicker baskets, canvas hoods, chains and great bundles of rope. Inside, a half dozen passengers were almost hidden by goggles, kerchiefs, burly overcoats, scarves, and lap robes.

This machine had scarcely thundered by (at a speed of almost fifteen miles an hour), when a second automobile appeared, also decorated with flags. Then came a third and a fourth. Every few seconds, there was another, until no less than thirty automobiles passed. Their destination was the Del Monte Hotel, over a hundred miles away. The distance would take less than eight hours of travel. The automobiles making the entire journey without their axles breaking or their engines exploding would be tenderly parked in a long row under the cypress trees while their owners ate a late lunch inside the Del Monte Hotel and exchanged motoring stories. Then it would be time to drive back to San Francisco.

The automobile transformed the ragged countryside south of San Francisco into a fantastic tapestry of baronial manor houses, ornamental gardens, rolling lawns and French chateaus.

Rancho San Mateo, 6,438 acres of the finest land on the Peninsula, passed from the Mexican governor Pico to Cayetano Arenas to William Davis Merry Howard, who built a cottage there before the gold rush. After Howard died, John Parrott and sea captain Fred Macondray took property there. Soon afterwards the mining and railroad barons began laying out estates, to the displeasure of the Athertons and the other old Peninsula families.

James Flood built a rambling white gothic house with steeples that his detractors called "Flood's Wedding Cake." Nearby, in Palo Alto, Leland Stanford laid out racetracks and stables for his thoroughbreds on a nine-thousand-acre farm. One hundred and fifty employees tended the horses, and he raised the nation's most expensive carrot crop to feed the colts.

In 1866 Anson Burlingame, on his way to China to be the American minister, visited William Ralston at Belmont. Ralston persuaded Burlingame to purchase 1,043 acres of land before he sailed. Burlingame returned only once to see his land before he died. At the time society discovered the mobility of the automobile, this land was still very much country, a patchwork of fields and ranches tied to the city by the thread of the Southern Pacific Railroad.

When Ralston died, William Sharon inherited Belmont. When Sharon died in 1885, Francis Newlands, a Yale graduate and successful attorney (married to Sharon's daughter Clara), inherited the mansion, the Palace Hotel, and Sharon's considerable real estate holdings, which by now included much of Burlingame's property.

A no-nonsense businessman, Newlands sold Belmont, because it was expensive to run. He fired the manager of the Palace Hotel, thirty cooks and nearly all the waiters. The remaining waiters were ordered to submit to searches when they went off duty and to shave off their mustaches. Then he turned his attention to real estate.

In the middle of Burlingame's wooded thousand acres, Newlands found a cottage where his father-in-law had secreted his mistress, Sarah Althea Hill, in happier days. Newland's eye transformed Burlingame's land and his own into a subdivision with Sarah Althea Hill's cottage as a clubhouse. San Francisco was filled with wealthy young men who had little interesting to do with their time. Here was a place where they could come to escape the San Francisco fog and sport about in the countryside. In the evening, Newlands saw them settling into a cozy house on a lot he had sold.

Newlands organized the Burlingame Country Club in 1893. Its first headquarters was a small house on Rudolph Spreckels' ranch. After Sarah's cottage was remodeled, the club moved to this twenty-acre property. One hundred and twelve men enlisted in the club, paying the thirty-dollar initiation fee and the thirty-dollar annual dues—a small investment to play the role of a country squire.

Since none of them knew exactly what a country squire was supposed to do, or what was supposed to happen at a country club, the first organized activity of the club was a Parcheesi tournament. However, as they read magazines and asked around, they learned that country club members were supposed to ride in steeplechases and hunt foxes, so they bought pink hunting jackets and laid out a course.

By 1897, they felt they had more or less mastered country living. Early on New Year's Day, carriages began gliding up to the porch of the cottage, which had been decorated with shrubs, potted flowers, and, for some obscure reason, Japanese lanterns and paper umbrellas. The men, in tweed suits, climbed down and greeted each other heartily, while the women, in long furs, examined each other critically before settling themselves in wicker chairs on the porch.

The first activity of the day was a pigeon shoot. The women sipped tea and chatted while the men, armed with expensive shotguns, cleared the sky of any unfortunate birds that happened to fly into the neighborhood. The destruction of each target was met with cheers and clapping. Then it was time for lunch, which was served on tables set with pots of violets.

After lunch the club's members and families traveled to a field down the road where a mile-long elliptical track had been laid out and set with ten hurdles for a steeplechase. A rather gaudy silver cup, donated by the

Duke of Abruzzi when he visited the preceding year, was the prize. Since it had been raining continually the preceding week, the field resembled Lake Erie. The club members valiantly put on their riding jackets, mounted their horses and tried (with little success) to get them to swim around the course. When a horse actually got to one of the hurdles and jumped over it, the other members and their wives applauded wildly.

When that event was done, it was time for the principal event of the day: the hunt. Walter Hobart bought thirty-eight foxhounds and had them shipped from New York; this was to be the first chase using real hounds on the Pacific Coast. With a terrific barking and yelping, the hounds charged off, pursued by the club members in pink hunting jackets, white breeches and black caps. They galloped across the green fields of San Mateo chasing not a fox, but a sack of aniseed dragged by a horse. After a long and hair-raising chase, they caught up with the sack of aniseed. The hounds were tossed a sack of stew beef to make up for their disappointment and the weary would-be country squires rode back to the clubhouse for cocktails, dinner, and a grand ball.

At the turn of the century, the strange Scottish game of golf was introduced. John Parrott laid out a three-hole course and each morning the members braved the stiff winds and got dizzy trying to swat the ball somewhere near the hole.

In 1908 the club members received a rude shock. The town of San Mateo, a village that lay along the Southern Pacific tracks, announced it was going to incorporate Burlingame within its city limits. For the Burlingame Country Club's membership, this was extremely upsetting. Barbarians from the outside could overrun their green pastoral paradise, build bowling alleys in their sylvan glades and run roads through their enchanted forest. They hurriedly convened to plan a defense.

Luckily, some of their members were among the best lawyers in San Francisco. Their solution was to incorporate Burlingame as a city, then San Mateo wouldn't be able to touch them. All they needed was a petition with the signatures of a majority of the people who lived around the Country Club. Soon San Francisco's best citizens were visiting the cottages and farmhouses that surrounded the Country Club, explaining to the inhabitants that they would be much happier as their own masters than as a remote province of San Mateo. If Burlingame was a city, they could have their own city hall, mayor, police car, post office, and anything else they wanted. The inhabitants were won over. Shortly after they signed, the city of Burlingame appeared on the map.

The members of the Burlingame Country Club scarcely finished celebrating this victory when, in 1910, they received an even ruder shock. Those kindly pensioners and farmers who had signed their petition incorporating Burlingame now formed the Burlingame City Council. They discovered that they could assess property taxes and were looking at the Burlingame Country Club. That was the very height of ingratitude.

There was only one way out. The members of the Burlingame Country Club, many of whom now lived near the golf course, were forced to collect signatures on petitions again. This time they didn't take chances; they collected only their own signatures. Before the year was over, the newest city of all, the tiny but proud city of Hillsborough, nestled against the boundaries of Bur-

lingame. Within its borders was the Burlingame Country
Club and the houses of its members.

The woods and fields of Hillsborough were soon filled
with truckloads of cement and brick and dozens of
carpenters and masons building castles and mansions for
the Golden Circle's members. They built Tudor manors
and Italian palaces. Even a Petit Trianon was built.
Called La Dolphine, it was only slightly larger than the
one that had belonged to Marie Antoinette. Richard
Tobin, whose father built the first great mansion on Nob
Hill, built a miniature Norman castle, complete with
tower, spire, and lily ponds instead of a moat.

Michael de Young, the editor of the *Chronicle*, somehow managed to arrive at the end of his life without
being assassinated. His place both at the *Chronicle* and
in society was taken by George Cameron, who married de
Young's daughter Helen. It seemed only fair to Helen
that she have a castle too. Cameron built her an enormous eighteenth-century Georgian manor of pink cement
which he romantically named "Rosecourt."

Templeton Crocker, the grandson of Charles Crocker,
already had a dark brown, four-story, thirty-six-room
Swiss chalet in Hillsborough, but he felt that wasn't
enough. In 1913 he built a gigantic steel, concrete and
brick bunker. This marble-floored edifice was an unfortunate marriage of a Babylonian pyramid and the Mag-
inot Line. He called it "Uplands."

Harriet Pullman Carolan, heiress to her father's invention of the Pullman Car, and her husband, Francis,
decided to build a French chateau in a great park. The
architect they hired was assigned to find period rooms in
France which could be pried out of their houses and
shipped to California.

By 1915, Carolands was more or less complete. On the outside it had the appearance of a Parisian bus station; it had cupolas, mansard roofs, balconies and rosette windows all over its enormous façade. Inside, of its ninety-two rooms, two were bodily lifted from France and the rest were careful imitations. It was surrounded by terraces, gardens, a teahouse, statues, acres of orchards, a bandstand, a picnic ground and a cement replica of the Palace of Versaille's Temple of Love.

The Carolans moved into Carolands and immediately discovered certain inconveniences. For one thing, the delicate French windows, designed for the gentle breezes of the Loire Valley, were not quite up to the gusts of San Mateo. When the wind rose above a whisper, the windows banged with the noise of an artillery barage. This same wind sought out the French chimneys and howled out the fireplaces, blowing gray storms of ash onto furniture and guests. Finally, when one of the ornate French toilets was flushed, the Niagara-like crash of water resounded in every one of the ninety-two rooms.

After seven months, Harriet Carolan gave up and moved to New York. Francis Carolan retired to Crossways Farm. Harriet returned a decade later with a new husband, but the toilets still sounded like Niagara Falls. She gave up, sold the furnishings, and moved out for good. The house was left to the wind for the next twenty-five years.

Romantic fantasies were not confined to architecture. San Francisco's business leaders applied their fantasies to the Bohemian Club.

The city's businessmen had a number of private clubs where they could retreat to smoke cigars and read their newspapers in peace. Shortly after the fire, the most exclusive of the clubs, the Pacific Union (formed by the merger of two clubs whose members' names dated from before the Civil War) took over the smoke-stained brownstone walls of James Flood's mansion on Nob Hill. An excellent chef was hired. The blinds were kept tightly pulled, and a discreet but firm man was put at the door to see that no woman entered the building. The only exception allowed was if a member had a heart attack and a nurse came with the doctor. That took care of exclusiveness.

But the leaders of San Francisco's banks and industries wanted something more. They wanted to feel they were more than mere clerks and tradesmen; they wanted to be thought of as princes of the West, as men who appreciated opera, but who could shoot a bottle off a shelf at twenty paces; as cultured frontiersmen who could recite poetry by George Sterling and swear like Wyatt Earp. It was no coincidence that the best-selling novel of the day was Zane Grey's *The Man in the Forest*—the story of a simple frontiersman who conquered the business and social worlds of New York and then returned home to the mountains of the West.

The businessmen began joining the Bohemian Club, a club founded in 1870 by Henry George and an odd collection of writers and artists to provide a place to sing, argue, and get drunk. When members reached a point of giddy intoxication, they sang offensive songs and acted out disrespectful skits they had written, to the accompaniment of great cheers and crashing beer steins.

In 1878 one of the Bohemians had the idea that they should have a grand outing. The others agreed. That summer they piled out of the city, loaded with blankets and whiskey, to a redwood forest north of San Francisco.

They had such a good time that they did it again the following year. They liked it so much that they bought a piece of forest, 280 acres of redwood trees along the Russian River.

As each summer passed, the outings became longer. Simple afternoon frolics became tradition. Lighthearted jokes lent themselves to ritual. As businessmen replaced artists, it became very important to be a member of the Bohemian Club. It was even more important that some men not be members. The club built an impressive red brick headquarters in downtown San Francisco.

When a real Bohemian, that is one from Czecho-slovakia, walked in the door, seeking companionship, he was told he was in the wrong place. Bohemia had been annexed by society.

In July the dusty country roads near Monte Rio on the Russian River were lined bumper to bumper with big touring cars. Inside them, squeezed among suitcases, crates of liquor, spears, suits of armor, furled banners and sleeping bags, were the men of San Francisco society, dressed in boots, old flannel shirts and battered army campaign hats.

When they reached a rude wooden gate, the cars pulled up to a field. With the help of numerous servants, the baggage was unloaded. The men walked into the shadows of the redwood trees greeting their fellow Bohemians and looking for their campsites.

In the middle of the three-hundred-foot redwood trees was a clearing where fallen trees had been planed and laid out as benches and tables. This was the dining room. A little further on, was another clearing where a large stage had been built among the trees.

Men scattered up the ravines. One hundred sixty small campsites were spread throughout the forest. The smallest of these had a rude stove and bar in front of a canvas tent. The most elaborate had a well-stocked bar, tended by a bartender and butler at the entrance of the tent. The "Green Mask" had ship's lanterns hung from the trees. A huge ice chest filled with liquor and covered with moss was tied to the tree branches. At "Pelican," thirty campers stood around a huge redwood stump that had been made into a bar. "Lost Angels," the camp for members from Los Angeles, was crowded with men cooking over a large grill. At "Tuneville," the members, all musicians, sat in a circle playing jazz. High up the hillside Earle C. Anthony, the Packard dealer for the state of California, was sitting under a tree. He had provided a Packard to any member who needed transportation to the grove.

While the members unpacked and greeted old friends, guests of the members wandered through the grove. They included governors, United States senators, diplomats and corporation presidents. Some of them wandered into a particularly elaborate camp called "Land of Happiness," where they were turned back by the icy stares and overly formal greetings of the members. Even in the Grove, there was a pecking order. One did not drop into "Land of Happiness," the camp of William Crocker and other of the wealthiest men in San Francisco, without an invitation. The guests hastened back to their own camps.

As darkness fell, word was passed that it was time for "The Cremation of Care." The members and guests walked through the darkness to the dining circle. They stood, quietly, over one thousand in number, waiting. This opening ritual of the summer encampment was the most solemn ceremony of the Bohemian Club.

Suddenly, faint music could be heard coming from

high on the hillside. A senior member stepped from the crowd and announced in a loud voice:

Bohemians, by the power of our fellowship, Dull Care is slain. Hearken! High upon the hill you may hear Care's funeral music.

The guests heard the dull tolling of a bell and the sound of Chopin's funeral march. They saw the flickering light of torches coming closer through the trees. A row of grim-faced men appeared. Some were carrying torches, others were beating drums and playing the funeral march, and still others were carrying what looked like a corpse on a stretcher. The members whispered to their guests that it was the effigy of Care.

After the cortege passed through the dining circle and into the forest, the senior member called, "Bohemians, follow to Bohemia's Shrine!" The members and their guests obediently followed the dark road into the forest. They emerged in a moonlit clearing beside a large pond and were directed to sit down. On the far side of the pond, under a huge and gnarled old tree, was an immense statue of an owl, the symbol of the Bohemian Club.

When there was quiet, the sound of soft voices singing could be heard coming from the trees behind the shrine. Then, a shadowy figure emerged from the gnarled tree and began to sing.

The shadowy figure, called the Hamadryad, vanished back into the trees, and the torches were extinguished, leaving the shrine lit only by moonlight. A man in a long red robe, accompanied by several other robed men, stepped from the trees to the front of the shrine. This was the High Priest.

The High Priest stepped forward, looked at the men across the pond, and shouted:

The Owl is in his leafy temple; let all within the Grove be reverent before him. Lift up your heads, O ye Trees, and be ye lift up, ye ever-living spires. For behold, here is Bohemia's shrine and holy are the pillars of this house. Weaving spiders, come not here!

The High Priest walked slowly to the edge of the pond and was joined by two robed men; he intoned a lengthy poem, which concluded:

Our funeral pyre awaits the corpse of Care.

An eerie fluting came from the woods. A small boat carrying the effigy of Care, poled by a single boatman, glided slowly across the pond toward the High Priest. Members who had seen the ceremony a dozen times watched intently. The huge audience was perfectly still. As the boat approached, the High Priest continued to solemnly intone.

The orchestra played a loud fanfare when the boat touched the end of the pond. The effigy of Care was seized and raised over the heads of the robed acolytes who carried it to the foot of the statue. Suddenly a loud crash interrupted the music. A spotlight abruptly illuminated a ghostly tree near the shrine. The acolytes put down the effigy, as if surprised. A loud voice, identified as the voice of Care, came from behind the ghostly tree.

Fools! Fools! Fools! When will ye learn that me, ye cannot slay?/ Year after year, ye burn me in this grove,/ lifting your silly shouts of triumph to the stars./ But when again ye turn your feet toward the market-place,/ am I not waiting for you, as of old?/ Fools! Fools! to dream ye conquer Care!

The High Priest walked down to the edge of the pond, looked sternly at the illuminated tree, and shouted:

Nay, thou mocking spirit, it is not all a dream./ We know thou waitest for us/ when this our sylvan holiday shall end./ And we shall meet and fight thee as of old./ Some of us shall prevail against thee,/ and some thou shalt destroy./ But this, too, we know;/ year after year, within this happy Grove,/ our fellowship has banned thee for a space,/ and thy malevolence that would pursue us here/ has lost its power beneath these friendly trees./ So shall we burn thee once again this night,/ and in the flames that eat thine effigy,/ we'll read the sign: Midsummer set us free.

But the voice of Care came again.

So shall ye burn me once again! Ho ho,
Not with these flames which hither ye have brought
From regions where I reign!
Ye priests and fools, I spit upon your fire!

At those words fireworks exploded near the pyre, and the torches which the acolytes carried went out. The High Priest fell to his knees in front of the huge statue of the owl, raised his arms, and cried:

O thou, great symbol of all mortal wisdom,
Owl of Bohemia, we do beseech thee,
Grant us thy counsel!

The orchestra began playing a dramatic fanfare. A glow of light came from behind the owl, silhouetting it. A lamp flared at the feet of the owl. A deep voice spoke:

No fire, if it be kindled from the world
Where Care is nourished on the hates of men
Shall drive him from this Grove.
One flame alone
Must light this pyre, the pure eternal flame
That burns within the Lamp of Fellowship
Upon the altar of Bohemia.

The High Priest rose to his feet, picked up a torch, and walked up to the lamp flaming at the foot of the owl.

"Great Owl of Bohemia," he said solemnly, "we thank thee for thy adjuration." He lit the torch from the lamp and turned toward the audience across the pond, saying:

Begone, detested Care, begone!
Once more we banish thee!
Let the all-potent spirit of this lamp
By its cleansing and ambient fire
Encircle this mystic scene!
Hail, Fellowship! Begone Dull Care!
Once again Midsummer sets us free!

The High Priest touched his torch to the effigy of Care. It exploded in flame, and the audience across the pond applauded and cheered. The ceremony was over. Talking and laughing, the crowd began walking back to the bars in their camps.

Throughout the following week, the Bohemians pitched horseshoes, swam in the Russian River, shot clay pigeons, walked through the woods, gossiped, told stories, and drank prodigiously. On the last evening, they watched the Grove play, a gorgeous spectacle of color, trappings, spear-carriers, dramatic processions and violence with a minimum of acting. The members wrote the plays and played all the parts, including the women's roles. The plays had titles like, "The Fall of Ug" or "The Atonement of Pan." Invariably, they ended with several hundred people milling about the stage in complete confusion to the crashing of a loud orchestra and the imperfect but melodic singing of a tremendous men's chorus.

Then, late at night, the members shared a final round of drinks and returned to their tents. Off in the woods, someone could be heard, singing at the top of his lungs, "Dan, Dan, the lavatory man, who spends all day in the old crapping can."

The next morning the Bohemians, weary but pleased with themselves, drove back to their San Francisco mansions and Peninsula estates, satisfied that they had once again proved themselves not mere businessmen, but "men of the forest."

10. THE GOOD CROCKER AND THE NAUGHTY CROCKER

As in every family, the Crockers had some people of whom they were very proud and others whose names they preferred not to mention.

The favorite Crocker was William Henry, the second son of Charles, the man who built the railroad. W.H., as he was known, was a short, plump man with a round face and a spade-like beard that gave him the look of a cheery Buffalo Bill. He was also, as president of the Crocker-Woolworth Bank, the richest man in San Francisco.

W.H. was born in Sacramento when his father was working on the railroad. As a consequence, he rarely saw him. His mother took firm control and saw to it that he was properly educated as the son of a great man. He was sent to boarding school in Switzerland and then to Yale. At the end of his first year at Yale, his father took him (with three of his college friends) on a three-week pack trip in the Sierras. When he graduated, his father offered him another pack trip and his mother offered him a trip to England. He took the trip to England.

W.H. returned from England in 1883. At that time, he sat down with his father to decide what he should do with his life. He was twenty-two. He told his father he thought he ought to go into business and his father agreed. His father asked what branch of business and W.H. said he had often thought about banking. That was a good business, his father said.

Not long afterward W.H., in a business suit, was sitting behind a desk in a large office in the building on Pine Street, whose sign read, "Crocker-Woolworth Bank." Men, surrounded by guards, unloaded five hundred thousand dollars in gold from a truck parked in front and carried it into the vault. Charles Crocker was a thorough man. He hired R.C. Woolworth from another bank where he was president and made him president of his bank to allay depositors' distrust of a twenty-two-year-old bank president with no banking experience. W.H. was given the title of Cashier.

Ten years later Woolworth died and Crocker became bank president. Like William Ralston a generation earlier, Crocker put his bank behind a dozen enterprises. He built the first hydroelectric plant in the state and built a railroad in the Sierras. He financed a sea captain named William Matson who wanted to start a shipping line. He imported mining engineers from South Africa to look for new gold mines in the mountains and helped build the city's new gas and electric company. As we saw earlier, he also financed the Parkside Real Estate Company and, without knowing it, employed Abraham Ruef as one of his attorneys.

He was a member of every club and a contributor to every cause. He was an active Bohemian, a member of the Burlingame Country Club, a founder of the San Francisco Opera and a leader of the Republican Party. His lively brunette wife, the former Ethel Sperry of Stockton, rebuilt a French village that had been destroyed in World War I.

Curiously, his special interest was astronomy. He financed expeditions by the Lick Observatory to Georgia, Sumatra, Egypt and Labrador. He went himself on expeditions to Australia and Russia, looking for an unknown planet within the orbit of Mercury. The explorers never found their unknown planet, but they did verify a new theory of relativity by a young German scientist named Einstein.

In 1930, after Dr. Ernest O. Lawrence invented the cyclotron, Robert Sproul, the president of the University of California, asked Crocker for the money to build a laboratory to house a newer, bigger cyclotron. In half an hour Sproul was on the ferry back to Berkeley with Crocker's check for seventy-five thousand dollars. The William H. Crocker Radiation Laboratory was built within the next year. Crocker's gift led to the discovery of tritium and plutonium, ingredients essential to nuclear energy and, eventually, nuclear bombs.

When Crocker died, he was mourned throughout San Francisco. A mountain in the Sierras was named for him. The family commissioned a biography, which was published in a handsome volume titled *Great Citizen*. The illustrations showed Crocker smiling, looking solemn and romping with his Bohemian friends. Unfortunately *Great Citizen* did not sell one-tenth as well as a book by another Crocker. W.H.'s niece, Aimee, published her book in 1936. Aimee was the Crocker the other Crockers tried not to think about. She called her book *And I'd Do It Again*. Following a photograph of a dark-haired woman, draped with pearls, looking seductively into the camera, the book began:

"I was born a Crocker of San Francisco. This is another way of saying that I had the golden spoon in my mouth. The Crocker family needs neither introduction nor comment. For those who do not read the papers, I might say that we were exceedingly wealthy."

After a brief description of her childhood, which she seems to have spent mainly on the waterfront in San Francisco, learning the language of sea captains, she went to Europe to be schooled.

"We went to one of those curious schools which Europe creates especially for American girls where you learn nothing at all of practical or educational value, but learn instead to act like a duchess, to flirt outrageously, to wear the clothes of a society woman ten years older than you are, to smoke, to drink and to carry on with the handsome young officers of the court. . . . to do a number of things that would make dear old Victorian mothers reach for their prayer books. . . . all in all, it was rather fun."

She promptly fell in love with a German prince with "the most romantic saber scars . . . and the most fascinating way of stiffening and clicking his heels together when he saluted you." She was engaged to him, and then broke it off. Next she fell in love with a Spanish toreador named Miguel and became engaged.

"He was brutal, conceited, childish, haughty, passionate, direct, and completely irresponsible. . . . He had seen admiration in my eyes. He flashed his teeth at me and flourished a bejeweled sombrero and waited for me to come to him.... I came all right. I made secret dates with him. I heard him through my ears, my eyes, my flesh, my pores.... saying phrases that sent maggots into my brain, poured brimstone into my blood ... his touch left scars on my soul. And when he kissed me, his breath proclaimed the fire that was to follow its vapor and bathed my body and heart in its madness while his hands gave off electricity.... Well, we will not go into the details of my puppy love."

This, when she was sixteen, brought the reader up to only page twelve. In the next eight pages, Aimee left Miguel, who was then gored to death by a bull. Next, she went to London, where she fell in love with the king of Hawaii. When she returned to San Francisco, she took her own apartment, secretly married a young socialite named Porter Ashe, and, on her honeymoon, was nearly killed when the train fell from a mountainside in the famous wreck of Tehachapi Pass. She decided the accident was a bad omen and divorced Porter Ashe, who went on to achieve some fame as Patrick Calhoun's lawyer in the post-earthquake bribery trials.

"I made up my mind that I was through with the people of my world," she said, "and with *civilized* life for all time. I would go away into the green, natural places where men are men and women are all hula-hula girls, and live my own life. In short, I would go to the South Seas."

Aimee arrived in Hawaii and met her old friend the king. Never one to relax, she began having adventures. She was attacked by a shark, went to a leper's ball on the island of Molokai dressed in a protective rubber evening gown, danced hula dances, was caught up in the middle of a revolution, and was nearly hypnotized by a sinister dwarf named Washington Irving Bishop.

Tiring of Hawaii, she married an American named Harry Gillig, and went to Japan. There her husband introduced her to an English diplomat named Huntingdon-Meer. Unknown to her husband, she became his mistress. Huntingdon-Meer introduced her to Baron Takamini, a Japanese who was immensely rich and "endowed with a singularly intense mind which had been developed at Yale, Heidelberg, and at the Sorbonne." Unknown to Huntingdon-Meer, she became his mistress.

Huntingdon-Meer eventually learned about Baron Takamini and fled to Bombay, and Baron Takamini, for reasons unbelievable even for this story, committed suicide. Harry Gillig evidently learned about both Huntingdon-Meer and Baron Takamini because he disappeared from the story entirely, and Aimee sailed on a ship for China.

For Aimee, it was a relatively uneventful cruise. Halfway through the trip, she observed an elderly Spanish gentleman who appeared to be quite ill with his young American wife. Before long the American wife came to Aimee and confessed that she was poisoning her husband. Aimee, who was naturally curious, asked why.

"I want his money," the woman said. "I married him for it five years ago, and he will never die unless I make him. Just that. No other reason." Aimee concluded, "Women have always been a mystery to me."

Arriving in Hong Kong, Aimee wasted no time. In less than two pages, she rescued the wife of a missionary from Ah Feng, "the owner of all the vice-dens in all the foreign settlements of China," and was herself abducted by Prince Huan Kai Chan. One of Aimee's British friends described him as a remarkable man, but a swine. Prince

Huan Kai Chan took her on his yacht to his house in Shanghai, where he entertained her by having a notorious bandit named Ling Wing-Pu diced in his courtyard.

" 'We have an amusing way in China, have we not?' he asked me. 'It is not given to every American woman to witness the Death of a Thousand Cuts.' "

Aimee did not find it amusing. She escaped from Huan Kai Chan in the middle of the night. Thereafter, he sent his servants to throw knives at her. This made for awkward moments, but fortunately for Aimee, they were poor shots.

"I would not have missed the experience of Huan Kai for all the world," Aimee reported. "But marry him? Never. Love him? Ridiculous. Admire him? Enjoy him? Well, I'm a woman...."

From Hong Kong, she traveled to Java. There in less than three pages she was kidnapped by Prince Djoet-ta, a headhunter from Borneo who had lately attended the funeral of Queen Victoria in London.

"I didn't know how else to do it," he explained. "You would never have come by yourself, and I want you to visit my country with me."

Aimee spent the next few weeks romping through the jungle of Borneo with the prince. When it occurred to her that he wanted her to be the Princess Djoet-ta, she declined. To the strains of the "Kanjor Dodo," the headhunting dance, the natives prepared to subdivide her. At that moment, the Prince announced he did respect her after all. He carried her, disheveled but unhurt, to an outpost of the Dutch Foreign Legion.

Next, Aimee took a ship to Bombay. In scarcely two pages, Aimee heard footsteps behind her and a bearded man tapped her on the shoulder and said: "If Memsahib will accept the compliments of my Master, the Rajah of

Shikapur, I, Poonga, am instructed to say that his house and his race will be honored above the stars."

"Mystery, mystery, mystery!" Aimee Crocker wrote.

"Adventure, adventure, adventure!"

Aimee wandered around India with the Rajah and, at her own request, lived for a week in his harem. "It was slavery and despotism," she wrote, "it was wonderful." But, other than one poisoning, an attack by a ten-foot cobra and a double murder, she found India rather tame.

When she returned to New York, Aimee brought a souvenir with her: a twelve-foot long pet boa constrictor named Kaa. Perhaps because of the old rivalry between San Francisco and New York society, or perhaps just because she had a rather odd sense of humor, Aimee invited fifty of New York's select to a dinner in honor of "H.H. Kaa, the Maharajah of Amber." Drawn by the title, the New Yorkers came.

"If I do admit it myself," Aimee wrote, "my entrance was superb." She wore a green evening gown made for the occasion and came in with her snake wrapped around her. She unwound the snake and placed him on the table in the center of the room. One guest fainted and another screamed and fled the room. The rest sat terrified in their chairs.

"It was very much fun," Aimee said. "The dinner was a great success, except that the newspapers picked it up and made the story into that of an orgy, based on some vague idea of snake-worship that was really impossible and very unkind." One suspects Aimee loved reading that story in the newspapers.

She filled the rest of her book with stories of her adventures among the famous and exalted people she knew. "I collect people as others collect postage stamps," she said. In two pages she dropped the names of Enrico Caruso, David Belasco, Diamond Jim Brady, the Barrymores, John Drew, Lillian Russell and Oscar Wilde. Wilde, she said, "was a frequent visitor at my San Francisco home.... I found Mr. Wilde a charming gentleman, fascinating as much for his courtly manner to women as for the pungency of his wit."

A scholar might rudely point out that Oscar Wilde only visited San Francisco once, and, according to the newspaper accounts, he stayed not at Aimee Crocker's house, but at the Palace Hotel. This same skeptic might express doubt about the truth of the stories of the toreador, Huntingdon-Meer, Baron Takamini, Prince Huan Kai Chan, the "Death of a Thousand Cuts," Prince Djoet-ta of Borneo, or even Poonga and the Rajah of Shikapur.

But even a skeptic might admit that if a person could take only one book on a long journey, he might prefer *And I'd Do It Again* to *Great Citizen*. Also, if he had to chose a companion at a dinner, he might prefer to listen to Aimee Crocker talk about being attacked by a cobra than listen to William H. Crocker talk about the Federal Reserve Board. We should be willing to forgive her if she exaggerated. San Francisco society has never been—and should never be—known for its modesty.

11. PROMENADE

Between the First and Second World Wars, San Francisco society lived its golden days. The city was the capital of the Pacific, drawing to it the wealth of all of Asia. The harbor was full of ships from Singapore, Tokyo, Shanghai, Java, Saigon, Hong Kong and all the fabled ports of the East.

Whether from their brick houses in Pacific Heights, the ballrooms of the hotels or their mansion in Hillsborough, the Golden Circle looked proudly on their city. They attracted the wealth, the power and the wit of the world. On a given day, you could find Somerset Maugham, John D. Rockefeller, Gertrude Lawrence, Noel Coward or the king of Saudi Arabia in San Francisco. Restaurants were second to none, the opera was excellent and the hills were magnificent.

For the first time, the Golden Circle were sure of themselves—sure of who they were and sure of their place. They all knew each other and at last they were known in New York. There was no more need to show off, no more need to marry their daughters to counts or princes or to have the biggest house with the highest tower. For the first time, it was enough to be a Flood, a de Young, a Crocker or a Spreckels.

The world was the garden of San Francisco society. They could stroll through it as if they owned it. Whether on long ocean cruises or month-long sojourns in Paris, Rome or Honolulu; whether in having tea with the society of Boston or New York or talking of their mutual friends, the Golden Circle had the satisfied feeling of knowing (really knowing for the first time) they belonged.

William Randolph Hearst, now sixty years old, owned twenty newspapers, a wire service, a feature syndicate, a newsreel company, a motion picture studio and more real estate than any man in California. San Francisco society and even New York society seemed small to Hearst. While they were content to build models of French chateaus, Hearst bought the real thing—had them taken apart and reassembled in California. While they were content to marry Vanderbilts or Pullmans, he married Millicent Willson in New York and then casually ignored her, giving his attention to a Hollywood starlet, Marion Davies. He was bigger than society and society resented it.

When he was first at the *Examiner,* Hearst lived quietly with a mistress in a cottage in Sausalito, across the Bay from San Francisco. His mother, Phoebe Apperson Hearst, learned about it and secretly visited the mistress. Soon afterward (and considerably richer), the mistress left Hearst. Hearst was distraught, but his mother, who took responsibilities seriously, lectured him on the fact that he was the son of a United States senator and her son—which meant he had certain responsibilities. Mrs. Hearst was a major patroness of the arts in San Francisco and the largest benefactor of the University of California, which had a Hearst Greek Theater, a Hearst Mining Building, a Hearst Women's Gymnasium and even a Hearst Avenue. She died in 1919, and William, who now had the money to do anything he liked, decided he would live the way he wanted.

He was looked down upon in New York and San Francisco society, but Hearst no longer cared. He would start his own society. His inheritance included a mountain resort near Mount Shasta, a Moorish ranch house, a ranch near Pleasanton, and a 45,000-acre ranch in the Santa Lucia Mountains by the Pacific halfway between San Francisco and Los Angeles. Here, in 1923, Hearst chose to build his castle. He instructed Julia Morgan, his mother's architect, to weave together the towers, ceilings, rooms and decorations he collected from buildings all over Europe.

Morgan constructed an astonishing one-hundred-and-fourteen-room castle with Moorish towers perched on a mountaintop. It seemed as if half the museums of Europe were squeezed into one building. English rooms crowded with French furniture under ceilings pried from Spanish monasteries were typical. A Greek temple stood beside his lake-sized swimming pool. Outside this was a private zoo stocked with giraffes, polar bears, eagles, kangaroos, leopards and Tibetan warring yaks. Zebras wandered freely on the grounds. Ex-presidents, oil executives, generals, foreign dignitaries and movie stars (everyone from Charlie Chaplin to Winston Churchill) were driven to San Simeon to dine in Hearst's medieval banquet hall. Hearst looked on these guests as his own private society. Looking around San Simeon, George Bernard Shaw remarked, "This is the way God would do it, if he had the money."

While Hearst was assembling his treasures, his newspaper rival was busy in the cultural garden of San Francisco. Michael de Young was the guiding spirit of the 1885 Mid-winter Fair, organized to rescue the city from its financial doldrums. It was such a success that de Young suggested the seventy-five-thousand-dollar profit be used for a permanent museum of art located in the fair's Egyptian-style fine arts building. Scarcely in the Hearst style, the de Young Museum was filled with miners' boots, mining equipment, sun bonnets and other relics of the Gold Rush. *Objets d'art* were allowed to accumulate until more space was needed, and funds were donated by de Young to build a new unit. Eventually, the museum became a full-fledged museum in Golden Gate Park, always connected with the de Young name, although it was operated by the city. The *Chronicle* never referred to it as "the de Young," but always as the M.H. de Young Memorial Museum, although it was not a memorial to Michael de Young, but to the Mid-winter Fair. For years, by editorial order, daily attendance was dutifully reported in the *Chronicle*.

Meanwhile, a third big family was entering the art field. Adolph Spreckels, whose poor marksmanship failed to kill de Young, was urged by his wife to build their own museum. They already had the most spectacular mansion in the city, a sugary white edifice on Pacific Avenue, with a great circular driveway. Like his brother, Adolph was an urbane, formal, independent and strong-willed man. When the noise of motorcars and wagons disturbed his sleep, he built large cement planters in the street. These were very picturesque, but they also made it impossible for a vehicle to travel faster than two miles an hour.

In 1908 he met and married Alma Emma Le Normand de Bretteville, the twenty-seven-year-old daughter of a working-class French family that claimed descent from Charlotte Corday, the slightly crazed aristocrat who tried to end the French Revolution by murdering Marat in his bath. Alma seemed determined to live up to her ancestor's reputation, and soon established herself as a woman to be reckoned with in San Francisco society. She had been an art student at the Mark Hopkins Institute, and helped rescue the paintings and sculpture from the 1906 fire. When she was eighteen, she posed for the statue of Victory which topped the Spanish-American War monument in Union Square. She rarely lost an argument, because, as one family member said, "she was tall, heavy and had a loud voice."

She was also a devoted admirer of France and French culture. When most of society's taste in art ran toward old masters and paintings of sad-eyed Irish setters, Alma was in France visiting Auguste Rodin, the father of modern sculpture. She liked his statues, which had been displayed in the French Pavilion at the 1915 Panama-Pacific Exposition in San Francisco. She bought one of the eighteen castings of "The Thinker" (shown at the Fair) and had it installed in Golden Gate Park. Then she decided San Francisco ought to have an entire museum devoted to French culture. The museum became known as the California Palace of the Legion of Honor.

Alma was known for her directness in raising funds for

her favorite charities. She once awakened Henry Ford at six thirty A.M. to ask for a Model-T as a raffle prize and got it. Now she devoted her energies to her museum. First, she needed a building. She decided to make it a memorial to the thirty-six hundred Californians who died in the war. This was part of her appeal for funds, but even this, she found, was not enough. People were not willing to give the kind of money she needed. Typically, she took the most direct approach; she went to the bank and borrowed the rest of the money on her husband's name.

She also needed Rodin's cooperation because she wanted as much of his work as she could get. She visited him in Paris and her friends visited him, but the elderly artist had doubts that the museum would ever be built. Then one of Alma's friends showed Rodin a picture of what she claimed was Alma's museum; it was actually a picture of Adolph's Pacific Heights mansion. Rodin was interested in the enormous house. A short time later, Alma got the sculptures she wanted.

Arrangements with the French government were made and soon workmen were swarming over the façade of the Palace of the Legion of Honor in Paris, taking measurements and making plaster casts of sculptures to be duplicated in San Francisco. Other men employed by Alma were going through the records and archives of the War Department gathering the names of the Californians who died in the war. Alma's relatives in France collected the signatures of Marshals Joffre, Foch and other French heroes for a memorial book to be given to the mothers of the men killed in action. She was thorough in everything she did.

On November 11, 1924, the museum was finished. It

dominated Inspiration Point, a cypress-bordered wind-swept bluff in Lincoln Park overlooking the Golden Gate. In the courtyard, Rodin's "The Thinker" looked toward the sea. Inside were French paintings, tapestries and furniture. Casts of Rodin's "Prodigal Son" and the "Age of Bronze," along with thirty-two other works, comprised the largest collection of the artist's work in the country. Alma bought the entire collection.

Before a large assembly of city officials, representatives of the French and American governments and the public, Alma passed out the black memorial books to the mothers of the men who had died. She, like them, was dressed in black, but she was not in mourning for their sons. Her husband, Adolph, had died only a few months before.

Alma inherited nineteen million dollars and the sugar cake house, but she was not one to play the reclusive widow. She was soon dominating every charitable event, most of which she organized. Her attention was directed more to the arts than society. The latter she left to her children.

Since Gertrude Atherton wrote *The Randolphs of Redwoods,* her own life followed the improbable course of the popular novel. She was reconciled with her grandfather and mother, but her husband George sailed to South America by himself. He was returned to Gertrude, pickled in a barrel of rum, the victim of a kidney stone. Despite her mother-in-law's admonition, she was determined to succeed as a writer.

"I no believe the womens can write," Dominga Atherton insisted. "If all were known, you find the mens write those books for them." Nevertheless, Gertrude left her daughter with Dominga and set out for New York to become a novelist.

"I had had enough of society," she said, "which seemed to me the most tiresome body of persons that could be gathered together, and I wanted to see something of that glamorous Bohemia of which I had read so much."

In a brief time she published two romantic novels. The critics were less than enthusiastic. "The abuse," she wrote, "was venomous, vituperative and personal, and some of the comments positively indecent." But both books sold well.

Encouraged, she began writing novels at a remarkable rate, finishing one in less than three weeks. She wrote novels set in ancient Greece, in Rome, in Washington, in Colonial America and in Spanish California. All were basically variations of *Randolphs of Redwoods*. When she found she could not write fast enough, she had high-frequency electric waves beamed at her pituitary gland. This not only permitted her to write faster, it also inspired her next novel, *Black Oxen,* a book about an elderly woman restored to youth by radio waves. *Black Oxen* was not only condemned by the critics, but by the medical profession and the church. It became one of the best-selling novels of the decade and her most famous book.

She was a celebrity. Samuel Goldwyn invited her to Hollywood as one of six eminent authors including Mary Roberts Rinehart and Elmer Rice. She dabbled at screenwriting and commuted regularly to Europe and New York, but she had no home. Dominga Atherton died, her grandfather and mother were dead and her daughter had grown up and married. The closest thing she had to home was the estate of James Phelan near San Jose.

After the dismal ending of the graft trials, Phelan retreated to his business. In 1915, when reform was again fashionable, he was elected to the United States Senate, where he served until 1921.

His eight-hundred-acre estate in Santa Clara County was named Montalvo. This miniature terrestrial paradise had a mountain, a small redwood forest, an outdoor amphitheater, a swimming pool (surrounded by little bathhouses), dripping fountains and a huge lawn decorated with a tiny Greek temple. The slight, gray-bearded Phelan retired there to enjoy his friends, including Gertrude Atherton, who visited him. Gertrude was given a room at the top of the stairs. Her balcony had a cushioned wicker sofa, an umbrella for shade and a table for books. The house was regularly busy with writers, artists, foreign visitors and Phelan's friends whom Gertrude shared. It was as open as the Atherton house had been closed. Finally, Gertrude found a place where she felt she belonged.

Phelan died at the age of sixty-nine in 1930. Gertrude Atherton lived until 1948 when, at the age of ninety, she died in the hospital on the campus of Stanford University.

In 1929, at the age of eighty-four, Lillie Hitchcock Coit died. In her will, she left money to beautify San Francisco, specifically with a monument to her firemen and a memorial to her husband, Howard. A statue for the firemen was made and placed in Washington Square. After considerable debate over what would be a proper monument, the city built a large, fluted column on Telegraph Hill and called it Coit Tower. When the tower was dedicated in 1932, one of the old engines of Knickerbocker Number Five was found, polished, and pulled to the base of the tower for the ceremony. Lillie's old fire helmet was placed on top of the engine.

In the same year, the venerable leader of San Francisco society, Mrs. Eleanor Martin, died at the age of one hundred and two. Patrick Calhoun, the president of the United Railroads until the stockholders removed him in 1913, owed the United Railroads $1,096,000. The new president accepted payment of one dollar and wrote the debt off as paid. In 1916 Calhoun declared he was bankrupt. He moved to Southern California in the early 1930's, invested in oil leases and made a new fortune. In 1943, when he was eighty-seven, he was killed crossing a street in Pasadena by two teenagers racing their cars. He was buried in South Carolina alongside Senator John C. Calhoun and Andrew Pickens Calhoun.

Eugene Shmitz's operetta, "The Maid of the San Joaquin," was panned by the New York critics, so he tried politics once more. After an unsuccessful effort to be elected mayor, he was elected to the Board of Supervisors in 1921 and reelected in 1923. When he died in 1928, the police and fire departments formed an honor guard at a funeral attended by the mayor and the board of supervisors.

Forbidden to practice law, Abraham Ruef went into real estate and investments. Humorously, he threatened to build an apartment house that would block Rudolph Spreckels' view of the Bay, but he actually developed the idea that the North Beach fishing docks could, with restaurants and shops, be made into a tourist attraction. Ruef was too early to get any profit from Fisherman's Wharf. He died in 1936, broke.

In the nineteen-twenties, Rudolph Spreckels earned

eighteen million dollars a year. Then the crash came. He lost the presidency of the First National Bank and declared bankruptcy in 1934. His bank was taken over by William Crocker's bank. He took his bad fortune as stoically as he had taken abuse during the graft trials. "Other financiers jumped from windows when they found themselves penniless," he said. "I never lost a night's sleep." He moved to a three-room flat in San Mateo where he died in 1958, at the age of eighty-six.

12. THE COW THAT GAVE CHAMPAGNE

As the 1920's began, Ned Greenway still guarded the entrance to San Francisco society, but the clamoring outside was becoming more and more insistent. San Francisco was booming. New wealth was coming to San Francisco every week, bringing with it new families who wanted their daughters introduced in society. Greenway attempted to limit his cotillion to the daughters of former members, but that only made the clamoring louder. Up until this time, only one woman, the extraordinary Tessie Wall, slipped through Greenway's precise standards.

Tessie Wall was the best-known madam in San Francisco. Her brothel was the most extravagantly decorated house in the city. "It wasn't that Tessie lacked taste," a salesman from Gump's, an expensive shop where Tessie shopped, said: "She had too much of it." Her house was decorated with acres of red plush, an enormous gold

Napoleon bed, draperies that once hung in the Spreckels home, a bedroom set from the Crocker's home, and a mirror and bedroom set from, of all places, the home of Mrs. Eleanor Martin. Above it all was a neatly embroidered motto: "If every man was as true to his country as he is to his wife, God help the U.S.A.!"

Tessie read the society page carefully every day. "Just what do you folks talk about at them society parties?" she asked one customer.

She soon developed an ambition to attend one of Greenway's cotillions. She bought more champagne from him than most of his other customers; she was, in fact, the only person in San Francisco who could drink more champagne than he could. She was known to have drunk twenty-two bottles in one night and had once outdrunk John L. Sullivan, the heavyweight champion of the world. Afterward, Sullivan sheepishly explained that he was used to beer, not champagne.

Greenway was one of her customers. She appreciated his social position, but not his particular aberration of using young boys to arouse him before he went to bed with one of her girls.

Greenway was unwilling to refuse a friend and a good customer, but Tessie's reputation was not of the sort he usually demanded from those on his invitation list. He compromised; Tessie was permitted to attend one cotillion dressed as a champagne bottle as part of the entertainment.

This only made Tessie more insistent that she be invited as a genuine guest. She badgered, pestered and coaxed Greenway until, finally, reluctantly, he gave in. Of the two hundred highly prized invitations to the 1911 Mardi Gras Ball, Tessie received one, but only, Green-

way insisted, on the condition that her name not appear
on the guest list, and thus in the newspapers.

The triumphant Tessie attended the ball on the arm of
her lover, a gambler named Frank Daroux, a man she
would eventually shoot and cry over. She entered the
ballroom of the St. Francis Hotel in a gown as fashionable as anyone's there, laden with an excess of jewelry.
This drew hostile looks from the women who knew who
she was and embarrassed looks from their husbands.
Daroux was uncomfortable and insisted they leave early,
but Tessie was radiant, dancing, sipping the punch, and
nodding gleefully at her acquaintances.

The next morning, Tessie looked at the society page.
Descriptions of the ball took up the entire page; the
decorations, the costumes and the entertainment were
described. In fine type, the names of the two hundred
guests were listed. As Tessie expected, her name was not
on the list. On the adjoining page, however, there was a
prominent advertisement:

REPORTED LOST

Tessie Wall reported to police early this morning the loss
of one diamond brooch, of great monetary and sentimental value, the gift of Frank Daroux. The loss is said to
have occurred somewhere between O'Farrell Street and
the Hotel St. Francis.

Greenway's home in the fashionable Richelieu Hotel
on Van Ness Avenue gradually became surrounded by
auto dealerships. If the honking and clatter of gasoline
engines that now invaded his quiet rooms wasn't bad
enough, his cotillion debs refused to be cowed in the
manner they once were. Greenway was forced, reluc-

177

tantly, to permit waltzing at his cotillions; even that wasn't enough. Signs posted in the ballroom warned members not to ragtime. There were also rumors that the girls and young men, instead of going home from his cotillions, went to the jazz halls of the Barbary Coast to dance.

Greenway died in 1924. He was scarcely buried when Paul Whiteman's orchestra took over the Civic Auditorium not far from the Richelieu. Jazz was played in front of a row of shiny new Model-T Fords. The Jazz Age arrived.

Horrified by this noise and disturbance, the Golden Circle retreated to the Mural Room of the St. Francis Hotel. Here, every Monday afternoon, far from the activity of Union Square and the traffic-filled streets, they placidly munched on salads, steak tartare and London broil, watched fashion shows, gossiped and warily eyed one another.

The Monday Lunch began as a pleasant afternoon diversion, but, with the passing of Ned Greenway, it assumed an importance far beyond that. It was important to be reassured that you were somebody, and to know exactly how much of a somebody you were. Ernest Gloor, the stern, Swiss headwaiter of the Mural Room, could let you know your importance in a second. In a short time, he replaced Ned Greenway as the absolute arbiter of San Francisco society. If he placed you at or near the first five tables inside the door, you were *in;* if he told one of his captains to lead you to the back of the room and hide you behind one of the pillars, you were *out.* On this account, much of the luncheon was devoted to head-turning. It was important to note who was advancing and who was being pushed back. Elaborate stratagems were devised to impress Ernest in order to get placed nearer the front. He was given expensive gifts, opera tickets, and dinner invitations to win favor, but he refused to be bribed.

All eyes were on the first five tables. Here, the matriarchs of society sat; their smallest gesture was noticed throughout the room. Audible murmurs could be heard when Helen de Young Cameron, the daughter of Michael de Young, rose from her front table and passed by the table of Alma Spreckels. Helen nodded to Alma. Alma nodded back and spoke to her companion: "Those de Young girls are nice, but we've never been close since my husband shot their father."

While the inner sanctum of society was ruled by Ernest Gloor, its outer reaches were patrolled by the society editors of the *Examiner* and *Chronicle*. Ultimately, they decided who was society and who was not. Accompanied by photographers with bulky cameras or (if the occasion was particularly opulent) by artists with large sketch pads, the society editors attended every event they thought important. Eventually, their presence or absence became the crucial factor in the success of any party or reception. When the editors left, they took with them a list of guests. The next morning, that list would appear in an imposing gray block of six-point agate type on the society page.

By reading this list, a hostess could discern who was acceptable in a given week. From it, she would make a guest list for her own party. Thus, the same guests appeared each week, reinforced by the society editors' lists published the next morning.

For someone outside society wanting to get in, this was an obstacle of considerable difficulty. However, if an aspirant gave a spectacular enough party, society would come. It had to be very spectacular, because San Franciscans had a reputation for excess.

The old guard remembered that Hermann Oelrichs celebrated his marriage to James Fair's daughter Tessie by giving a "Southern Swamp" dinner at the Pacific Union Club. The centerpiece was a jumble of rocks with a stuffed eagle perched for flight on the summit. In addition, the table was piled with moss, brush, oak branches and a stream of running water populated with real frogs, lizards and harmless snakes was contrived to flow in the center of the table. Bushes and ferns placed around the table were wired with tiny electric bulbs that winked like fireflies.

Harriet and Francis Carolan celebrated the completion of their Crossways Farm by having a party inside the stables. Guests were transported from San Francisco to Burlingame on chartered Pullman cars, each decorated with flowers and potted plants. When they arrived, they found the grounds ablaze with the light of five thousand Japanese lanterns and three thousand electric lights. Lights outlined the house and the stables, searchlights lit the patios, and a multicolored chandelier illuminated the inside of the stables. Wires had been strung to Redwood City, San Mateo and even Palo Alto to get the power for this illumination. Women draped with flowers and men in hunting coats supped outside the stable and were entertained by Spanish dancers and a Japanese ballet.

William Randolph Hearst's mother, Phoebe, transformed her country house near Pleasanton, a mock Moorish palace named Hacienda del Pozo de Verona, into an Egyptian garden for a party for a University of California egyptologist. A blue pavilion, calculated to resemble desert sky, covered the courtyard, palm trees were set in the corners and servants were dressed as slaves. An orchestra played music from *Aida* while each guest received a cartouche ring or a simulated Eye of Horus amulet.

The *Chronicle* described a party given in 1915 for Lincoln Beachey, the aviator renowned for flying upside down:

"[Beachey] was carried into the dining room hanging head downward from a chair. Guests wearing glasses turned them around and wore them on the backs of their heads. The feature of the meal, which began with dessert and ended with soup, was roast duck served upside down. Beachey climaxed the affair by trying to eat while standing on his head."

These events were tame compared to those of the 1920's. On February 12, 1922, society gathered at the Burlingame Country Club. Here, Templeton Crocker, Rudolph Spreckels and John Drum were among the two hundred guests. The men put on paper jockey hats and the women put on rainbow-colored paper leis tied with ribbons of flowers. Led by Joseph Tobin, the husband of Michael de Young's daughter Constance, they waltzed around the room, guided by young ladies who held the ribbons like reins. Helen de Young was there with her husband George Cameron as was her sister Phyllis and her sportsman husband, Nion Tucker.

The waltzing stopped so the guests could dine. When the orchestra took its place again, the guests began tapping their feet to the music. What the orchestra played was definitely not Strauss; it was Jazz. Enchanted, the Spreckelses, Tuckers, Crockers, Drums, Marshall Madisons and others began awkwardly dancing

181

to the new music. Soon the whole room was filled with frantic motion. Society moved into the Jazz Age.

Costume parties had long been the rage. The Carolans inaugurated their Parisian-bus-station mansion with a costume ball where Mrs. Walter Hobart came as a stork wearing a plain white gown, wings, and close-fitting cap with long bill. Ned Greenway came in the scarlet costume of a toreador. In 1917, the theme of the Mardi Gras was "The Court of the Czar." Guests dressed as Romanovs, counts, cossacks and gypsies attended. The ball, preceded by a lengthy Russian supper, was followed by the announcement that the real Czar had been overthrown in Petrograd. But, compared to the costume parties of the twenties, these affairs were nothing.

The restored Fairmont Hotel was the setting for the 1924 "Quatr'z Arts Ball." Here four jazz orchestras and no less than three thousand guests, dressed as mandarins, carrier pigeons, buddhas and gypsies, gathered. The papers reported: "Mrs. Loller, Jr.'s costume represented the California Poppy, with a yellow silk bodice studded with rhinestones and yellow ostrich plumes around the bottom of the skirt."

In 1925, this event was exceeded by the "Gold Ball." The Civic Auditorium was draped with gold cloth. Guests, costumed in what were supposed to be California themes, appeared as Indians, Spanish senoritas, gold miners and oranges and grapes. "Mrs. Horace Hill and Miss Marion Ziel were costumed as white leghorn chickens.... Mrs. Clinton LaMontagne was a state highway sign, in cloth of gold with a pointed hat, carrying a red signal light."

It was a time of grand impersonation. A banker with a few turns of silk and a painted mustache could be turned into a pseudogypsy. The swimming pool of the Fairmont, with the addition of painted poles, colored ribbons and gondolas, was turned into the Grand Canal for a Venetian Water Carnival. In Burlingame, a hotel clerk managed to turn himself into a member of society.

San Francisco society found itself being entertained at El Cerrito, a thirty-five-room mansion with its own chain of lakes that never seemed to be full. The host, a handsome young man with dark eyes and curly black hair, wearing a lavender-trimmed suit, introduced himself as Rex St. Cyr.

St. Cyr's wife, Jean, who was twenty years older than he, watched him possessively. In her sixty years, she had collected two fortunes. In 1879, she married the immensely wealthy William Rhinelander Stewart. She divorced him and married James Henry "Silent" Smith, the richest bachelor in New York. He died shortly afterward.

Possessing most of both men's fortunes, Jean Smith wintered at the Breakers in Palm Beach, a fashionable resort in 1915. There, on the beach, she saw a handsome young man wearing a pink bathing suit, accompanied by a Russian wolfhound. Later in the lobby of the hotel, she was told he was in mourning; he wore a black crepe hat, black trousers with white stripes, white shoes with black trim, and a handkerchief with a delicate black border. It was said that the young man came from a prominent French family and had been married to the late Mrs. Alexander Redfield, a very wealthy Connecticut matron. His name was Rex St. Cyr.

She arranged an introduction. Soon the graying widow and the young widower were having tea and strolling together through the lobbies of the great Palm Beach hotels. Three months later, the newspapers announced that they were married.

Reporters from William Randolph Hearst's New York *Journal-American* competed fiercely with reporters from the New York *World* to discover or invent sensation or scandal. Both sides sensed more than a story here. Reporters hurried to Hartford, Connecticut, where St. Cyr and Mrs. Redfield had lived. Telegrams were dispatched to France and to the papers' bureaus around the country in an effort to find out more about the young man.

The reporters' instincts were correct: there was a story. St. Cyr, they discovered, was not St. Cyr; he had been born Jack Thompson in Waco, Texas. When he was twenty-five, he went to New York where he worked as a hotel clerk and as a salesman in a department store. He practiced to hide his Texas accent and (with the help of his department store job) had been able to dress quite well. The name St. Cyr was adopted from one of the guests at his hotel.

By being in the right place at the right time, he met the very wealthy seventy-year-old Caroline Redfield. Mrs. Redfield liked St. Cyr and hired him as her personal secretary.

Not long after St. Cyr moved into the Redfield mansion, Mrs. Redfield was visited by a young millionaire friend named Alfred Livingston and his young traveling companion, Robert Swem. Mrs. Redfield enjoyed the lively entertainment provided by the three young men; the house was filled with laughter and parties. When her husband died, Mrs. Redfield invited Swem to join her and St. Cyr in the mansion.

St. Cyr and Swem soon developed a more than

friendly relationship. This upset Alfred Livingston. After tearful and bitter arguments with Swem, the youthful millionaire committed suicide.

St. Cyr and Swem now had the run of Mrs. Redfield's mansion. They bought an extravagant automobile and hired a Japanese valet and a French chauffeur. Swem began calling himself "Von Swem." When Mrs. Redfield died, St. Cyr inherited a good portion of her fortune.

What Jean Smith St. Cyr thought of this when she read it in the newspapers is not known. She did find that by marrying St. Cyr, she also acquired Swem. Now calling himself Burroughs, Swem joined them on the train from Palm Beach to San Francisco.

The threesome entertained San Francisco society in grand style at El Cerrito. When Jean Smith St. Cyr died not long afterward, she left her fortune to her husband. The entertainment at El Cerrito became even more lively. There were huge dances and late suppers. At a Persian Ball, one of the guests, George Pope, Jr., dressed as a Persian prince, rode his horse into the ballroom. When he tried to stop the horse, it reared and slipped on the polished floor, tumbling the rider into the crowd of guests. Pope was picked up and the horse was shooed out, and the party went on.

When the depression began to encroach on his fortune, St. Cyr married Mrs. George Carter, the widow of the governor of Hawaii and the heiress to the Kodak fortune. He even persuaded her to buy El Cerrito from him. She divorced him in Reno in 1940 and St. Cyr moved to Los Angeles. Here, even without a house, he lived in splendor. When he died, his home was the penthouse of the Biltmore Hotel.

In 1937, when he was fifty-eight, Swem, or Burroughs,

eloped with Mrs. Nellie Stetson Oxnard, a seventy-three-year-old heiress to a San Francisco sugar fortune, in her chauffeur-driven limousine. They established themselves in the Oxnard mansion in Pacific Heights where Burroughs amused society by talking about his wife who was too deaf to hear him. When she died, she left him her entire fortune. When Burroughs died in 1959, at the age of ninety, he left the fortune to his protégé and adopted son, an Arizona boxer named Frank Bostock, whom he had managed to get listed in the Social Register.

By the 1930's, this gay life began to get out of hand. There was too much champagne, too much dancing and the music was too loud. What had seemed giddy and exciting in the twenties now made the room spin. In the twenties, the fun promised to go on forever; in the thirties, it seemed as if it might all be over tomorrow. It was time for a last fling.

The Malcolm Whitmans (Jennie Crocker) hung their ballroom with huge comic strips. Guests came as Popeye, Little Orphan Annie, Dick Tracy and other characters from the funny pages. At another Burlingame mansion, society knelt in the ballroom to watch a turtle race. At the wedding reception of Isobel McCreery and Augustus Taylor, Jr., in 1937, guests were astonished when a plane flew overhead skywriting, "I love you." That same year, when the Roger D. Laphams celebrated their thirtieth wedding anniversary, two men in police uniforms stormed in and handcuffed Lapham and his banker friend, Herbert Fleishhacker. The men were led away. Suddenly, the "policemen" stopped, took off the handcuffs and burst into song. It was all a gag. The cops were members of a prominent glee club.

In August, 1933, motor launches carried society out to

the battleship *Pennsylvania,* anchored in the Bay. When they climbed on deck, they found the ship covered with marigolds. Hedges bordered the walkways, small waterfalls showered from the bridge, rock gardens decorated the hatches, flower beds (temporarily transplanted from Golden Gate Park) made the main deck a garden while musicians played atop the gun turrets.

Elsa Maxwell, a leading international party-giver who claimed she was born in a box at the San Francisco Opera, gave a Barn Dance at the St. Francis Hotel. Society, dressed in blue jeans and calico skirts, entered the ballroom to find a complete replica of a barnyard with a country store. Live goats, a horse, two pigs, a donkey and a cow (all looking very bewildered) roamed the ballroom. A country-music band alternated with an orchestra playing reels and waltzes from a stage at one end of the ballroom. At the other end of the ballroom, guests gathered around a replica of an old well filled with beer standing beside a full-sized mockup of a cow whose udder, when the teats were squeezed, spurted champagne.

13. THE LAST TANGO

Those nights in the Mural Room [St. Francis Hotel] were the end of our generation's F. Scott Fitzgerald era ... Betty Grable singing with Ted Fiorito's band, Perry Como sounding like Bing Crosby with Ted Weems ... opening nights were jammed and de rigueur.

> Music of the 1930's, from Herb Caen's
> *One Man's San Francisco,* 1976.

Henry "Hot Lips" Busse was playing for dancers in the Palace's Rose Room ... Eddie Fitzpatrick's band and the elegant dance team of Harger and Maye were the attractions at the Music Box.

> Dec. 6, 1941, from Herb Caen's *Don't
> Call It Frisco,* 1953.

San Francisco was hit hard by the financial panic of 1929, but the structure of society withstood the shock. Some lost millions but they had millions left, so it didn't matter. The Monday Luncheons continued in the Mural Room of the St. Francis, despite teams of WPA workers, breadlines and union pickets outside the hotel.

Mrs. James L. Flood, daughter-in-law of the Silver King, gave a dance for her son Jimmy in the terraced ballroom of her stone mansion in Pacific Heights. It was a finale for the Floods. Afterward, Mrs. Flood gave the house with its marble foyer to the Convent of the Sacred Heart and moved to a penthouse at the Fairmont. In the next block, the mansion of her sister-in-law, Jennie Flood, became the property of Miss Hamlin's private school.

Alma Spreckels gave a grand debut for her daughter, Dorothy, in the sugar cake mansion on Pacific Avenue. While the young people danced, Alma kicked off her shoes and curled up on one of her French sofas with a pitcher of martinis to watch the fun.

Mrs. Robert Hayes Smith was not so lucky. Her family's fortune disappeared and her limousine was repossessed. She clung to her mansion, even though she was unable to have the roof patched when it began to leak. She also refused to miss a Monday Lunch, even if it meant the humiliation of arriving in a taxicab.

Fortunately, she was a trusted friend of William Randolph Hearst. She was privy to one of his many personal scandals, this one involving the death of a prominent Hollywood personality. The publisher had promised her a job if she ever needed money. Sue Smith swallowed her pride and approached Hearst. He promptly hired her, and, for the rest of her life, she received two hundred and fifty dollars a week as a society writer for the *Examiner*.

Since she couldn't write, she usually farmed out her column to friends with literary ability. Her son, Nicol Smith, one of the organizers of the San Francisco Bachelors, was a frequent contributor. When she wrote the column herself she filled it with the parties of the de Young sisters so often that they said they preferred to read the *Examiner* rather than their own *Chronicle*.

The editors of the society section of the *Examiner* soon discovered that she repaid obligations to friends by mentioning them in her column. This was all right as long as the news was social, but when she mentioned a friendly pawn shop where she had hocked her jewelry, the item had to be deleted. Even though she was frequently ill and the leaking roof forced her to put an umbrella over her head when she sat in bed with her telephone calling for news, she never missed a deadline.

Her benefactor, Hearst, also had his troubles. In 1938 auditors walking through a warehouse on 143rd Street in New York marveled at the contents piled to the rafters around them. There were suits of armor, medieval stained glass, complete rooms from Elizabethan and Tudor houses in England, Mexican saddles studded with silver, the stones of old castles, Egyptian mummies, Greek statues, and crates containing Gainsboroughs and Rembrandts. All of them belonged to William Randolph Hearst.

Other auditors were making lists of the artworks and furnishings stacked in the two-acre storeroom under Hearst's castle at San Simeon, and still others were sorting through Hearst's belongings in the Haslett Brothers Warehouse on the San Francisco waterfront.

The auditors were there because William Randolph Hearst was flat broke. His imperial spending had finally outrun his imperial income. His name was attached to seventy-two companies which drew in fifteen million dollars a year, but Hearst spent all that and more in his quest to buy a large part of Europe and have it moved, whole or in pieces, to California.

He was the terror of his newspaper offices. If, at eleven o'clock at night, he saw something he wanted in the window of a San Francisco antique store, he quickly drove to the office of the *Examiner*, had someone wake up the owner of the shop and drive him downtown, taking enough money from the cash drawer to buy it.

The board of directors of his newspapers, exasperated by his spending, gradually began picking up his notes and taking control of his business operations while he toured Europe or entertained at San Simeon. In 1937 they politely informed him that they, and not he, owned Hearst Consolidated Newspapers. He was removed from the executive office and given the honorary title of Editorial Director. Auditors were sent out to catalog his possessions and hopefully sell them.

Hearst carried on as if nothing at all had happened. He celebrated his seventy-fifth birthday in 1938 in the rambling white beachhouse in Santa Monica that he built for Marion Davies. Marion Davies stood by his side as three hundred Hollywood celebrities, in costume, sang happy birthday to him. Dressed as James Madison, Hearst received his guests.

When the two bridges across the Bay were completed, San Francisco threw itself into a celebration. The Golden Gate International Exposition on Treasure Island opened in February 1939, holding a shining promise for the future of San Francisco. The U.S. Steel Pavilion featured a model of San Francisco in 1999: clusters of sixty-story skyscrapers towered over the capital of the Pacific. Another aspect of the future was demonstrated in the nearby General Electric Pavilion, where a model pressed two hundred shirts a day with an electric iron. Amid the gardens, fountains and statues of the fair, the Golden Circle held court at the Yerba Buena Club—an assemblage of gold lattices, yellow velvet drapes and sundecks overlooking a lagoon and a sunken garden. Mrs. Henry Potter Russell, the daughter of W. H. Crocker, was the president of the board. Considered a model of the new society woman, Mrs. Russell was concerned less with diamonds and Parisian gowns than with a host of committees, boards and causes. The club hosted a dinner for the most celebrated women in California. Among them were the author Kathleen Norris; tennis star Helen Wills Roark; the president of Mills College, Dr. Aurelia Henry Reinhardt; Congresswoman Florence Kahn; an enormously rich society woman whose hobby was leading expeditions to the north pole, Louise Boyd; architect Julia Morgan; and, of course, Gertrude Atherton.

Across the fair at another club, Pacific House, Mrs. William Denman and Inez Macondray Lundborg served tea daily to foreign envoys visiting the exposition. San Francisco society was on the summit; they were in those happy months, the hosts to the world, the proud nobility of a golden kingdom. Mrs. Denman and Mrs. Lundborg had difficulty with only one guest. No one wanted to talk to him. He was Captain Fritz Weidemann, the Nazi consul-general to San Francisco.

When Weidemann first arrived, the Germans bought a fancy house on Floribunda Drive in Hillsborough, and their consul settled there. At first, since he was a pleasant man, he was very popular there. He drove his Mercedes to parties in the city and on the Peninsula and was honored at a dozen receptions. Then, slowly, things began to change. The invitations began to drop off. The flag outside his office was torn down. Pickets appeared outside the office. Finally, one day in September, 1939, he locked himself in his office and left word he was not to be disturbed.

That day a headline on the front page of the *Examiner* announced: WARSAW BOMBED! GERMANY INVADES POLAND!

Within a year the fair closed and the buildings were

taken over for a Navy base. Warships crowded the harbor. Threatening headline followed threatening headline. San Franciscans began to realize, whether they liked it or not, that they were tottering on the brink of something terrible.

On December 7, a quiet Sunday morning in 1941, much of society was listening to a radio broadcast of the New York Philharmonic when a newscaster broke in: "We interrupt this program to bring you a special news bulletin. President Roosevelt said in a statement today that the Japanese attacked Pearl Harbor."

The golden dream was over.

For four years, San Francisco was the front. Temporary wooden barracks stood across from the Opera House. Hundreds of soldiers were quartered in temporary plywood cubicles in the Fairmont, St. Francis, Palace and Mark Hopkins hotels. The city was the embarkation point for thousands of soldiers and marines who sailed across the South Pacific to invade Guadalcanal, Tarawa and Iwo Jima. Thousands more came to San Francisco from the Midwest and South to work in the shipyards and armament factories.

The four San Francisco dailies went to war. Office windows were painted with blackout paint and the society writers were kept busy following the war relief and Red Cross activities of society. Mrs. Paige Monteagle ran the Stage Door Canteen to entertain servicemen on their way to the front. Mrs. William P. Roth put aside the collection of blue ribbons and horse show trophies her harness ponies had won to become head of the Red Cross Volunteers. Alma Spreckels organized a salvage shop in her garage that raised one hundred seventy thousand dollars for the Red Cross. Her San Francisco League for

194

Service Men provided a seemingly inexhaustible supply of radios, baseball bats, footballs and washing machines to the soldiers on every front. They also provided musical instruments for no less than one hundred seventy-six military bands. Phyllis Tucker, the daughter of Michael de Young, was president of the American Women's Voluntary Services.

Society not only sent washing machines and band instruments. Nion Tucker, Jr., Phyllis Tucker's only son, was killed in the Pacific. After her son Charles, Jr., was killed, Mrs. Charles Kendrick buried her grief by working as a Red Cross volunteer. Her daughter Geraldine quietly enlisted in the women's branch of the Marine Corps.

Fearing that a Japanese submarine might shell his castle, William Randolph Hearst took Marion Davies to the safety of his mock Bavarian village at Wyntoon, near Mount Shasta. From there he telephoned instructions and directives to the staff of the *Examiner* in San Francisco.

The fashion editor of the *Examiner* was given the assignment of buying Miss Davies' clothes at I. Magnin's. She carefully followed the telephone instructions as to style and size and sent the clothes by car to Wyntoon. To her surprise, they came back without an explanation. Then, the fashion editor realized Miss Davies was ordering the size she used to wear, not her present size. With the cooperation of the staff at I. Magnin's, she arranged to have a new lot of clothing assembled. This time, tags reading size fourteen and size sixteen were removed; tags reading size eight and size ten were substituted. The clothes were sent to Wyntoon and this time were not sent back.

Once, however, the staff balked. Prudence Penny, as

the food editor of the *Examiner* was called, received a request from Marion Davies to create a birthday cake for William Randolph. The request was accompanied by an architectural drawing of a cake in the shape of Mount Shasta, complete with trees, streams, and animals—all made of sugar. Because of wartime restrictions, sugar was rationed.

The food editor took the request to the office of Bill Wren, the managing editor. "This can't be done," she wailed. "There aren't enough sugar stamps in San Francisco."

Wren studied the drawing and suggested that the mountain could probably be scaled down somewhat. The food editor asked where the stamps would come from. Wren instructed her to simply collect them from the staff.

The staff of the *Examiner* would willingly alter the facts of any story for Hearst, but giving him their sugar stamps was another story. Unable to pry any from the staff, Prudence Penny was forced to wangle what she could from the Red Cross. For his birthday that year, W.R.H. received a small round cake with a single red rosette.

For four years, society was just another part of the war effort, raising money, entertaining soldiers, and wearing their uniforms to the Monday Lunch at the St. Francis. Then, for two glorious months in the spring of 1945, San Francisco society was able once more to play the role they played in 1939: host to the world. The State Department announced San Francisco had been chosen as the site for the charter conference of the United Nations.

Frantic preparations for the conference began. Delegations from each of the nations to be represented began demanding preferential space from hotels already over-crowded with soldiers. Housing had to be found for three thousand visitors. The government charitably raised its restrictions on alcohol so the delegates could be enter-tained in a traditional San Francisco fashion. Accom-modations had to be found for twenty-five hundred reporters.

When the conference opened on April 25, twenty-seven flags flapped over the entrance to the St. Francis Hotel and more flags flew over the Mark Hopkins and the Fairmont. Lurline Roth recruited her Red Cross volun-teers to act as ushers. For San Franciscans, who had been facing a grim, colorless war, it was glorious. The men they had been reading about for four years were suddenly right among them in San Francisco.

Suddenly the Russians were not a faceless ally in a comic strip or on a poster, but were present in the person of V. M. Molotov, the People's Commissar for Foreign Affairs, with his trim gray mustache, rimless glasses, humorless smile and poorly-tailored plain black business suit. The British were perfectly represented by the tall, slender Anthony Eden, with his pink face, clipped mus-tache and quiet Oxford accent. Georges Bidault, Charles de Gaulle's foreign minister, looked just like the French resistance leader Humphrey Bogart played opposite in *Casablanca,* which San Franciscans had seen the year before. Edward Stettinius, the white-haired former chair-man of the board of U.S. Steel, looked as though a Hollywood casting department chose him for his role as the secretary of state.

Most spectacular of all were the Arabs, who swept through the lobby of the Fairmont in white robes and jeweled scimitars, awing the crowds that came to see them. One Arab called to his admirers, "You should see me on a horse!"

The Golden Circle was overjoyed that, at last, they could give and attend parties without their being considered a needless extravagance. These were a vital part of the war effort.

Because of her experience as a hostess at the 1939 World's Fair, Helen Russell was chosen as the hospitality chairman of the conference. She promptly organized no less than 550 official dinners and 240 cocktail parties, costing over a million dollars. A typical banquet for 810 guests at the Palace Hotel consumed 257 bottles of Korbel champagne, 1,980 cocktails and $300 worth of cigars and cigarettes in a few hours. When they were not drinking champagne at the Palace, the delegates were being wooed by the Arabs, who took over the de Young Museum for a night to offer bourbon, turkey, and twelve kinds of salad. The Russians offered them vodka, prawns, oysters and platters of herring. When the delegates were not eating red herring, the U.S. Navy took them on blimp rides over the Bay and the Army took them on drives to Muir Woods. When they were not looking at redwoods, the Golden Circle invited them to Hillsborough and Pacific Heights for more oysters and cocktails. Hostesses boasted of the number of prime ministers or foreign secretaries they had at their parties.

Every guest list had to contain at least one celebrity. Lord and Lady Halifax, Senators Vandenburg and Connally (whom the reporters nicknamed Tweedledee and Tweedledum), Nelson Rockefeller (who, from the most expensive suite at the St. Francis, was assigned to keep the Latin American delegates happy) and the handsome secretary-general of the conference, Alger Hiss, were all lionized by the Golden Circle. Everyone tried to get Molotov and the Russians, but they seldom left the St. Francis or their rented mansion retreat in Hillsborough. Next to Molotov, the most sought after guest was Anthony Eden, but he was quickly captured by Betty Flood, the wife of Jimmy Flood (grandson of the Silver King), who kept him at her parties in Woodside. Unfortunate hostesses chose their guests from the leftover delegates or the assistant deputy foreign ministers from unfashionable countries or minor American delegates, such as Adlai Stevenson.

The final party of the conference was given by Nelson Rockefeller at the St. Francis Yacht Club. Mayor Roger Lapham was a guest of honor. A tall, handsome man with a thick shock of white hair, the Harvard-educated shipping magnate and millionaire member of society seemed the picture of the way San Francisco saw itself. As the party reached its peak, Mayor Lapham, in evening dress, was in the center of the dance floor, trying valiantly to tango with Carmen Miranda.

14. THE CHROME CIRCLE

After the war (WW II) we danced to Swing music . . . we
learned the Cha-Cha and Rhumba from Carmen Miranda . . . and there was a lot of what we called
"Staggering Music," we just hung on to each other and
went around the floor.

> Mrs. Jackson Schultz
> of Hillsborough, a member of
> the Cotillion Committee

When the United Nations Charter was signed on June
26 and the delegates finally went home, San Francisco
society was content. They had proved themselves cosmopolitan. They had chatted with the leaders of fifty
nations and shown them their mansions and clubs. They
were the salon of the world. The city of San Francisco
confidently applied for the position it felt it earned, the
permanent home of the United Nations. A few months
later, shortly after the end of the war, the Golden Circle
was stunned and angered when the United Nations
announced it would locate its headquarters in New York.

More shocks followed. For decades San Francisco
dreamed of surpassing New York, of becoming the capital of the Pacific. At the 1945 United Nations Conference
the goal seemed within reach. But commerce and politics
work in their own ways, unaffected by sentiment. The
commerce went to other places: Seattle, Portland, Los

Angeles and even Oakland—which had better railroad connections to the rest of the country.

The business community was determined to stay in the race with New York, whatever the cost. After the earthquake of 1906, they rebuilt San Francisco from a collection of wooden castles into a modern brick business city. Now, it appeared, if they wanted to compete with New York, they would have to rebuild a financial center of steel and glass towers, computer centers and international consortiums. "You've got to live modern," said Ben Swig, the owner of the Fairmont Hotel. "You've got to think big to be big. The whole San Francisco skyline is going to change. We're going to become a second New York."

The cost was high. San Francisco was once a town of castles on hilltops, a small golden kingdom between the Ocean and the Bay, where everyone in society knew everyone else. William Randolph Hearst or Rudolph Spreckels or William Crocker were recognized when they walked down the street. All this would be lost. San Francisco would become just one more connection in the corporate grid, one economic block interlocked with a dozen others. Its executives would be interchangeable, transferring from New York to Chicago to San Francisco as their corporations required. Neither they nor San Francisco could afford to be unique. Its architecture must look like New York—cold and modern; its airport must look like any other airport. Above all, its suburbs must be indistinguishable from New York's or Chicago's. An executive must be able to move from Westchester to Winnetka to Hillsborough without suffering needless shock; his wife and children must be able to find wives and children just like themselves.

202

In 1954 the Burlingame Country Club decided they needed a larger clubhouse. They selected "New Place," the rambling mansion which had belonged to William H. Crocker, but they didn't have the money to buy it. Once, they would have sought a donor like Crocker or Spreckels or Hearst, but now in the middle of a corporate community filled with dozens of men who wanted to use the club's golf course, that was impractical. Instead, they simply voted to increase membership by fifty; each new member was charged a five-thousand-dollar initiation fee. They quickly had enough to buy their new clubhouse.

The great estates south of San Francisco were being closed in by real estate developments. The houses being built were not ordinary tract houses, by any means; they were large, modern, ranch-style houses, set on at least an acre of ground, designed to house the executives of the new corporate San Francisco. One by one, the great estates were carved into lawns, swimming pools and cul-de-sacs. The estates around the white-towered Flood House, Linden Towers, became a development called "Lindenwood." The twenty-acre estate of George Pope in Hillsborough became "Elmwood Gates." The huge lawns and gardens that surrounded Carolands, that great, windy, abandoned Parisian bus station, were fenced and houses built. The estates that remained were scattered green islands in a great sea of driveways and ranch houses.

Country houses passed into other hands. Henry Crocker's ranch near Cloverdale became "Slim Dunlop's Covered Wagon Dude Ranch." Phoebe Hearst's Moorish palace at Pleasanton, Hacienda del Pozo de Verona, where she and her guests had played at being Egyptians under a painted blue sky, became the clubhouse of a golf course. At San Simeon, tourists gaped at the marble swimming pool and baronial banquet hall of Hearst Castle. It was now a state park.

In 1951, the eighty-eight-year-old Hearst was sharing a house in Beverly Hills with Marion Davies. At the instruction of his doctor, she entertained him each night by talking with him about their friends and the parties they had had at San Simeon. Early on the morning of August 14, 1951, he dozed off in the middle of their conversation. She got up quietly, left his room, and went to her own room to go to bed.

Shortly after dawn, a nurse went into Hearst's room to see how he was and found him dead. She hurried out to get his sons, William Randolph, Jr., and David. Richard Berlin, the president of the Hearst Corporation, and a doctor were also called. The doctor examined Hearst, signed the death certificate, and an ambulance took the body away. No one bothered to wake Marion Davies.

When she woke up, she recalled, "I asked where he was, and the nurse said he was dead. His body was gone, whoosh, just like that! I was alone, old WR was gone, the boys were gone. Do you realize what they did? They stole a possession of mine. I loved him for thirty-two years and now he was gone. I couldn't even say good-bye."

She was not even invited to the funeral, for Hearst belonged again to San Francisco society. A crowd of fifteen hundred waited outside Grace Cathedral on Nob Hill during the funeral service. There were two hundred floral displays and a message of condolence from General Douglas MacArthur. Governor Earl Warren sat in the pew behind Hearst's five sons and his widow, Millicent.

One by one Hearst's collection of artworks was auctioned off to help pay the debts he had piled up. A group of Flemish tapestries was donated to the de Young Museum. To the astonishment of the elders of society who had savored the violent rivalry between the two families, it was decided to put them in a "Hearst Court" in the center of the museum.

Because of the Marion Davies affair, which was certainly the worst-kept secret in social history, the Hearsts were not in the Social Register. They saw the dedication of the "Hearst Court" as an opportunity to let society know of their presence.

The *Examiner* treated it as a news event of approximately as great importance as VJ Day. An advance task force of reporters and photographers was sent to the museum to review the preparations and bring back scouting reports. Meanwhile, the entire Hearst family, led by the publisher's widow, established themselves at the St. Francis Hotel. Bill Wren, the managing editor of the *Examiner,* studied his advance task force's report and examined photographs of the tapestries. He summoned his photographers for a final briefing and instructed them not to take any pictures in front of the tapestry of Adam and Eve in the Garden of Eden, since they appeared not to be wearing clothes.

On the night of the dedication, both the society reporters and the news reporters were given a police escort to the museum. When the event was over, the reporters hurried back to the *Examiner* office to write their stories. All the photographs of the Hearst family were taken to the St. Francis Hotel to be approved by the family. The entire newspaper—art, engraving, editorial and circulation—awaited the family's verdict. Finally the word

205

came: the group photograph of the family was all right, except for William's son, David. Another picture of David's head was found in a hurried search through the *Examiner*'s files, it was pasted onto the family portrait, and the *Examiner* went to press.

The summer encampment of the Bohemian Club now looked more like an international business conference than a wilderness outing. In 1959 the members and guests sat by the side of the pond to listen to lectures by Arthur Summerfield, the attorney general of the United States; Grayson Kirk, the president of Columbia University; General Carlos Romulo, the minister of education of the Philippines; and former President Herbert Hoover, all attired in baggy trousers and sports shirts.

Many members of the Bohemian Club arrived at the Grove in private business planes. The Grove changed considerably since the rough days of the twenties; there were now telephone booths, a barbershop, a hospital, a post office and a grocery store. The members could sleep under electric blankets and sip cocktails from plastic cups with the seal of the camp on them. Even the Cremation of Care had been modernized; the effigy of Care was made of flammable Styrofoam.

For not a few members, the Grove presented a chance for an extramarital fling. Some wives were told the outing lasted six weeks, instead of three. Prostitutes put the dates of the encampment on their calendars and set up shop in motels in Rio Nito and Guerneville, while society writers speculated on the number of heart attacks that might result.

Not long after the war, skiing replaced horseback riding as the favorite pastime of society. Because it could only be done at distant places, was expensive, and most of its nuances and rituals could be enjoyed without actually taking the risk of putting on skis, it made an ideal sport for the Golden Circle. The comfortable wooden houses that circled Lake Tahoe and served as bases for boating parties on the lake in summer, now became winter ski lodges. Ski racks appeared on the roofs and backs of the Golden Circle's cars. Sugar Bowl, a ski resort in the Sierras, became a frostbitten outpost of the Burlingame County Club where San Franciscans built new lodges to spend their weekends near the slopes.

The skiing enthusiast's finest hour came in 1960 when the Winter Olympics were held in Squaw Valley. The almost unknown California resort was chosen through the personal politicking of Alexander Cushing, a tall, snobbish Harvard graduate who searched California for the perfect site for a ski lodge after World War II and built it with the aid of the Rockefellers and other Eastern financiers.

The financial backers came West for the Olympics and worried through days of rain, which washed away the parking lot, before snow finally fell. While Eastern society provided the money, the West provided the entertainment. Prentis Cobb Hale, Jr., was chairman of the games and Mrs. Richard Walker was hospitality chairman. Everyday parties were held for Prince Bertil of Sweden, and the dozens of other international notables at the Games in the Sierra. San Francisco silent film star William (Buster) Collier and his wife, Stevie, a beautiful, one-time Ziegfeld showgirl, entertained constantly in their apartment at Squaw Valley Lodge (which they had to rent for the entire year to make certain they would have it during the Olympics).

The Squaw Valley success inspired hundreds of Californians to go to Innsbruck, Austria, for the 1964 Winter Games, but they missed the compact Sierra Valley where all the events were within walking distance. Many stayed in Innsbruck hotel rooms and watched the contests on television. By 1968 the thrill was gone. Only the most die-hard ski enthusiasts went to the Winter Games in Grenoble.

Even that most venerable institution, the Monday Lunch at the St. Francis, was shaken by the changes in San Francisco. Ernest Gloor made sure that only the old guard, in their neat suits, gloves and hats, dined at the first five tables inside the door. Beyond that, all was chaos.

Angelina Alioto, a small woman with bleached blond hair, came from Dallas to marry Joseph Alioto, a balding and successful attorney from a large North Beach Italian family. When she saw that belonging to San Francisco society meant being at the Monday Lunch, she pleaded with her husband for a table. After negotiations that rivaled the United Nations conference in complexity, Alioto prevailed. At the next Monday lunch, Angelina had her table. It was not one of the first five, but neither was it in the back of the room, in "Siberia." Both halves of the room glared at her with resentment. For the first few weeks, she sat alone. From then on, she brought her daughter Angela Mia with her. Angela Mia sat on the floor and together they glared back. Whether society liked it or not, Angelina Alioto was one of them.

But the days of the Monday Lunch were almost over. There was little time to arrange hats and put on gloves and much less to spend at long luncheons in a dark hotel.

In 1959 Ernest Gloor died. His place was taken by a similar-looking man named Barney, but Barney did not have the unerring judgment of his predecessor. When it came to table placement, one veteran Monday-Luncher complained bitterly, Barney "made a number of serious mistakes." Tables emptied. Soon, the room came to resemble a dark museum; even the chicken salad tasted musty. Many of the diners moved a few blocks away to Trader Vic's, where, if one's social importance was not equally honored, at least the atmosphere was cheerier and the food better. In 1962 the St. Francis ended the Monday Lunch. A few years later, the Mural Room itself was demolished and the lobby, now crowded with businessmen and conventioneers, expanded in its place.

Since the Opera House was completed in 1932, opening night at the opera was the major single event of the social season. Box seats were passed from generation to generation by the members of the Golden Circle. This was the occasion used to display their full array of jewelry and furs. Mrs. Milton Esberg, Jr., invariably wore the jeweled topaz tiara that had once belonged to the Empress Eugenie. Dorothy Spreckels, Alma's daughter, always wore her fifteen-thousand-dollar platinum mink coat. The women stepped from their limousines at the carriage entrance and advanced through the foyer like empresses. One woman marched into the Opera House in a cape of real carnations that made her look like a float in the Rose Parade. By the end of the evening curious opera-goers had plucked almost every flower from the cape. Another grande dame trailed a furry train that slithered after her like a pack of small weasels. A spectator, fresh from the bar, watched with fascination.

"My God! What is that?" he asked.

"Sables, young man," she snapped, "and damn good ones!"

But even this sacred institution was shaken by, of all

people, the San Francisco Giants when they moved to San Francisco in 1958.

San Franciscans regarded the acquisition of the Giants as a major triumph. At last they had taken something away from New York. Perhaps they were gaining after all. Policemen on street corners wore Giants caps. The chauffeurs of limousines wore Giants caps. Behind the chauffeurs, the titans of San Francisco commerce wore black business suits and black Giants caps.

Some men gave up their opera tickets for Giants tickets. Tallant Tubbs said, "I've heard *Lucia* several times and know what happens, but I don't know how the Giants and Cubs game is going to turn out."

In the San Francisco Opera House, the patrons of the opera, listening to Anna Moffo singing in *Lucia di Lammermoor,* heard a peculiar tinny buzzing. They looked around and realized that many of the people in the boxes were listening to the Giants game on transistor radios.

Tallant Tubbs, the heir to a cordage fortune, was a favorite extra man in society and a devout Giants fan. He brought elegant lunches from the Pacific Union Club to eat in his box next to the dugout at Candlestick Park. At the grand opening of Candlestick Park, the sailing segment of society decided to go by yacht to the ballpark which adjoined the Bay. Headed by Dan London aboard his sleek cruiser, *Adventuress,* the little flotilla of yachts sailed south with the enthusiasm of the Spanish Armada, and the same unfortunate results. Getting the yachts to Candlestick Park wasn't difficult, but getting San Francisco's elite (wobbly from their maritime adventure and a great many cocktails) onto dry land proved to be a major undertaking, accomplished only after a great deal of shouting, gesturing, and near-disasters. Hilary Belloc, the son of the great English author, was rushed to an emergency hospital to have a finger, nearly severed in the mooring, sewn together. Then he was rushed back to the ballpark.

When the Duke and Duchess of Windsor came to California on their first and only visit (with Cadillac, station wagon, trailer, dogs and servants), Tubbs managed to get them to stop over in Phoenix to watch the Giants during spring training. The duke and duchess then went on to Pebble Beach where, in keeping with their tradition of staying with friends and not at hotels, they stayed with Elizabeth Fullerton Coleman.

Elizabeth came from Miami, Oklahoma. She met another Miamian, George Coleman, the owner of a considerable number of oil wells and part of the Pittsburgh Pirates, and married him. Then, pursuing the sort of social glory Oklahoma didn't offer, she convinced him to move to Pebble Beach. By making the friendship of Winthrop Aldrich, a former chairman of the board of the Chase Manhattan Bank and ambassador to the Court of St. James's, she succeeded in getting herself in both the Burlingame Country Club and the Social Register. Before long the proud mother was able to announce the engagement of her oldest daughter, Ann, to a member of New York's Woolworth family. She consulted the society editor of the *Examiner* on each step of the procedure.

This was the beginning of Elizabeth's breathtaking social ascent. She left Coleman behind and married W. W. Crocker, the son of W. H. Crocker, which put her very near the summit of San Francisco society. The rest of the Crockers were not especially pleased. When W.W. died, they fought the will, and succeeded in keeping her daughters from the Crocker fortune.

It didn't seem she could advance higher, but she did.

Near her Hillsborough estate was an estate belonging to the Duke of Manchester, a descendant of the duke who had visited San Francisco society in his boots and mining shirt. This duke had considerably broadened the family fortune. Thanks to his wealthy American mother, he owned several houses and an estate in Kenya. His Australian wife was in poor health. When the duchess died, Elizabeth was the first to arrive at the duke's house with flowers and condolences. It was not long before the widow from Miami, Oklahoma was the new Duchess of Manchester. A new title hunt, a sure sign of social insecurity, was soon underway.

Elizabeth had the grandest, but not the only title in Hillsborough. Dale King Christenson, ex-wife of a wealthy lumber scion and a very rich woman in her own right, married Vicomte de Bonchamps. Her niece, Mildred Cowgill, who once worked as a San Francisco society writer, married the Marquis de Surian. Both couples spent most of their time in Paris making annual visits to San Francisco.

Much earlier, Helene de Latour, whose French parents founded Beaulieu Winery, married the Marquis de Pins and acquired a French chateau that belonged to his family. Her daughter, Mrs. Walter Sullivan, Jr., became honorary consul to Monaco, a position that didn't involve much work due to the shortage of Monacans in San Francisco, but was very nice when Princess Grace and Prince Rainier and their two older children visited San Francisco.

The former Genevieve Lyman was so fond of her second husband, Italian Prince Ranieri di San Faustino, that she kept her title of princess although, in her real estate business, she used plain Genie. The prince was not skilled in the art of earning a living and his wife, one of society's true charmers, found her niche. Ever wanting to advance upward socially by moving to a new address, San Franciscans kept buying and selling their increasingly expensive Pacific Heights homes to each other. It was very chic to have the wife of a prince as your saleswoman. Genie's close friend, the former Edith Macy, made it clear that she and her husband, Karl Schoenborn, were just Mr. and Mrs., no nonsense about his title of count, although they did enjoy visiting his ancestral castle in Austria. Edith's mother, Mrs. Roland Redmond, of New York and Santa Barbara, was married to Prince Ranieri before he married Genie—if you want to keep the record straight. Karl Schoenborn once worked as a taxi driver, but finally his talent as a perfect gentleman was discovered by Tiffany, and he wound up an executive of the jewelry firm.

No one can dispute the title of Prince and Princess Vasili Romanov. He was a nephew of Nicholas II, the last czar of Russia. Vasili was sent to Denmark as a child during the Revolution and eventually came to the United States, where he met and married his beautiful Natasha. San Francisco society took them to its heart. They had style. No one could smoke a cigar at the cotillion with the aplomb of the Russian princess. Prince Vasili, who tried various ways of earning a living, eventually became a successful stockbroker. Their daughter Marina has "princess" listed with her name in the New York Social Register, but neither she nor her husband, William Beadleston, the art dealer, use it. However, they named two of their children Nicholas and Alexandra.

San Francisco's other link with nobility is David Pleydell-Bouverie, the younger son of an English peer, who lives as a gentleman farmer in the Valley of the Moon, the rustic haven in Sonoma County made famous by Jack London. Bouverie was once married to Alice Astor, a lucky match, although it ended in divorce. Alice's brother, Vincent Astor, is supposed to have told David that he made his sister happier than any other man and presented the Englishman with a million dollars. Bouverie's ranch was bought with the proceeds and on any given weekend, the handsome blond host, in Levi's and boots, can be found entertaining an array of house-guests ranging from visiting titled gentry to writers like Shana Alexander. Assorted San Franciscans, among them Anton LeVay, head of the San Francisco Satanic Church, who puts on a good act at being sinister, are also guests. Bouverie, a patron of the arts, has served on the board of trustees of the Palace of the Legion of Honor. His farmhouse, a tribute to his background and taste, is filled with Georgian silver and eighteenth- and nine-teenth-century paintings, including portraits by Sargent.

In a sugar cake white mansion above Pacific Heights society lingered on in the person of Alma deBretteville Spreckels.

Alma, almost six feet tall and brandishing a glare that could turn salesmen and waiters to stone, had not changed with the times. As the years passed, she out-glared, outshouted or simply outlived all of her rivals. She labored mightily at her social tasks; she summoned the director of her museum at all hours of the day and night to praise or berate him. She toured Europe for the Labor Department to study the condition of working women. "I used to be a stenographer and I'm proud of it," she announced. She donated paintings and statues and built buildings everywhere.

She aged, but she did not slow down. At three o'clock in the morning, she could be found walking through the Palace of the Legion of Honor, examining the paintings, dressed in a nightgown and slippers covered by a mink coat. Visitors to the sugar cake mansion were summoned to her bedroom where they found her imperiously settled in a four-poster bed ornamented with carved swans. In that bed, she informed them, kings had made love. Propped up by pillows, she conducted her business and read mystery novels until she felt it was time to play bridge. Then she put on her slippers (she never wore anything on her feet except slippers), got out of bed, and went to one of the bridge tables which were located everywhere in the house, including each of the house's twenty-six bathrooms. If she felt an urge to go swimming, there was a pool in her own garden. There the eighty-two-year-old Alma would take off her clothes and go skinny-dipping.

Eventually, Alma became a recluse. Accompanied by a nurse and chauffeur, she would climb into a dark blue Buick sedan for a drive through San Francisco and the suburbs. She first circled Union Square and looked at the statue of herself as Victory on the top of the Dewey monument. As the mood moved her, she would then cross the Golden Gate Bridge to leave a gift, usually a mystery novel, at the home of her brother. Sometimes, she would cross the Bay Bridge to stop outside the Berkeley house of her grandson, Adolph Rosekrans, or would visit another of her numerous relatives scattered around the Bay. She rarely saw her relatives; usually, she waited outside in the car while her chauffeur delivered a present. On certain extraordinary occasions, however, she would announce that she wanted to talk to her relatives, who would be telephoned and warned that she was on the way.

They would be waiting dutifully by the curb when Alma's car arrived. The electric window hissed down, and the relative was instructed to lean his head inside the car and chat with Alma who was seated in the back seat. "You knew, when she finished, she'd just press the button on the electric window," one relative recalled fondly. "You had to get your head out of there *very* fast."

Society in the 1950's was trying so hard and growing so fast that there was little room for uniqueness, and less time for picnics. There was a great deal of money, a great deal of snobbery, and very little imagination or grace.

In 1956 the Golden Circle asked Stanley Peters, an English interior decorator who had done work for the royal family, to visit San Francisco and participate in the Tour de Decor. This fund-raising scheme for the Museum of Art was an event where international decorators arranged rooms for society women, in appropriate costume, to sit in.

Peters had heard a great deal about San Francisco, the cosmopolitan meeting place of Asia and the West. He accepted the invitation and it was arranged that he would be hosted by a different part of society each night. Peters arrived in San Francisco, saw the Tour de Decor, then eagerly went to his first society party. He was greeted by eight couples in black tie and evening gown and given a dinner. Afterward, they played bridge.

The second night, he appeared at his new host's home and was confronted by eight more couples, some the same as the previous night, all in evening dress. Once again they had supper and played bridge. The third

night, he arrived at the home of attorney Turner Mc-
Baine and his wife and, to his dismay, found the same
eight couples smiling at him. After supper they went to
the bridge tables. Peters looked around, put down his
cards, and said, "You're all ghastly bores! I didn't travel
six thousand miles to play bridge." He got up, walked
out of the house, took a cab downtown, and checked into
a cheap hotel.

The society editor of the *Examiner,* hearing what
happened, tracked him down. "I haven't had a chance to
see the real San Francisco," he complained. "I've just
been passed from couple to couple as a houseguest. They
are nice enough, but it got pretty boring. The same little
tables on either side of a large sofa. The same big coffee
table with the latest books and magazines laid out. I
want to meet the artists, bohemians and San Franciscans
in other walks of life. In London, you'll find a duchess
enjoying a conversation with a penniless artist."

Regrettably, it was true. San Francisco society had
become as bland and faceless as the steel and glass office
buildings downtown. The glitter and excitement and
excess of the Hearsts and Aimee Crocker were gone.
Costume parties and banquets had been replaced by
cocktail parties and buffet suppers. But it was a time of
startling change, and a new kind of society, made for
those times, was coming.

15. THE SHORT FLIGHT OF THE JETSET

Indoors or outdoors, any place can provide a dance floor
for the hippies, who think that they are undulating in
motion with the universe, expressing joy and well being.

Time, July 7, 1967

The jetset took off on the soaring Dow Jones averages
of the early 1960's. They were the new people, the
beautiful people, who took pride in the fact that they
wore the newest clothes, went to the most fashionable
ski slopes and gave the best parties. You never quite got
to know who they were, or why they were special,
because you saw them for only a moment before they
were off to somewhere else. They were always smiling
and apologizing that they had a plane to catch.

Sometimes they tried to get into the established circles
of society, but for the most part they didn't need to.
They were like gypsies camped outside the city gates.
The rulers of the city looked down on them with disdain,
but the rulers' children were sneaking out the back gate
to join their dancing.

San Francisco became the capital of the counterculture. A shabby neighborhood, where Haight Street intersected Ashbury before running into Golden Gate Park, was becoming a shrine for thousands of young people. Drawn by newspaper and television stories and word of mouth, they heard that something special was happening there. The people, it was said, had freed themselves; they wore flowers, passed out free food, slept together, created visions with drugs, and nodded into reveries listening to stereo record players blaring loud and haunting music they called "acid rock."

There was a "counter" to everything, in fact. Opposing traditional poetry were a dozen bearded and humorless poets in North Beach, turning out pages of bitter and, they hoped, obscene anti-poetry. Opposing traditional religion was a host of mystical cults, largely imported from India or Japan, promising various sorts of deliverance. Odd churches and temples sprang up in different parts of San Francisco. Opposing the Brooks Brothers suits and short hair of the Montgomery Street businessmen and the elaborate coiffures and neat suits of the women shopping at Magnin's came a whole fashion cult of bushy hair, Nehru jackets, colored beads, velour and satin jackets, wire-rimmed glasses and bell-bottomed trousers that made parts of San Francisco look like a Cecil B. De Mille vision of an Oriental bazaar.

There was a new language, with a considerably reduced vocabulary that depended heavily on the words "man" and "far out." New movies, new paintings, new breakfast cereals, new everything was the rule. It did not matter if something was better, as long as it was new. Of course, little of it really was new, but it certainly was different.

It followed that there had to be a new society, freed of convention and restraint. In the beginning of the sixties, it was simple; all you had to do to be avant-garde was live with someone without marrying. Joan Hitchcock, a brunette with a magnificent figure, didn't resort to granny glasses or long skirts; she got all the attention she needed in a low-neckline dress. Shortly after she came from Chicago, she caught the eye of Peter Hitchcock, the son of an enormously wealthy Golden Circle family with an estate in Woodside. Soon the two of them were living together in Sausalito. Hitchcock's ambition was to triumph in the world of polo. Unfortunately, he was a perfectly awful polo player. He found he could best play polo vicariously by generously funding the teams that played on the Peninsula.

Joan's ambitions were more worldly; she wanted to be one of the people the world paid attention to. Living in sin in Sausalito was a good start, but it wasn't enough. She convinced Peter it was time to marry and to buy an enormous mansion in Pacific Heights, which Peter bought. In a short time, the invitations were flying out in all directions. Joan had what she wanted: her new ballroom was crowded and she, in a low-cut gown, was the center of all eyes. She had arrived.

But it was not enough. After a while, she and Peter split up. Peter stayed on in the mansion on Outer Broadway while Joan and their two children (plus two children of a previous marriage) moved to another, almost as grand, house on Broadway which had belonged to Virginia Hobart, the daughter of a Bonanza king. Virginia, whose marriage to Charles S. Baldwin gave her national social prestige, married a bankrupt Russian prince, Zourab Tchkotoua after Baldwin died. The young prince vanished from San Francisco, but she kept his title. To the waiters at the Monday Lunch at the St.

Francis she was thereafter known as "Princess Choo-Choo." Joan continued to hold endless parties in the new house on Broadway. A second husband and a third disappeared, but Joan was not dismayed. The parties went on. Late one night at a noisy gathering, she bumped into the society editor and a photographer for the *Chronicle*. She saw them notice her cleavage (of which her gown left little to be imagined). She slipped her breasts from the gown, displaying them to the photographer, and said proudly, "They got me three husbands. They'll get me more."

Joan got married so many more times that the press lost count of the number. Peter died, leaving ample support for his sons, but that was all the money Joan had, even after she sold off various pieces of real estate she owned. Lack of money never stopped Joan from giving parties. She was a survivor—unlike some of the other young women of this flamboyant jetset era.

The Golden Circle was making as much news as the jetset. Some spent more and more of their time in court to defend their fortunes. Heinrich Kreiser, the German butcher, had come to San Francisco in 1850 and changed his name to Henry Miller. He put together a cattle ranch, moved to South Park and was one of the richest men in California when he died in 1916. His estates and ranches extended from Mexico to the Canadian border and together were twice as large as Belgium.

Court battles for his estate began shortly after he was buried. California and the federal government tried to seize his ranches as inheritance taxes. After eleven years of courtroom argument, they were stopped by his daughter. Next, the estate trustees were charged with fraud and conspiracy. This case took ten years and fifty-three lawyers to settle. In 1965, forty-nine years after Miller died, his forty-million-dollar estate was finally divided evenly between the two branches of Miller descendants, the Bowleses and the Nickels. The Nickels protested that there were more of them than there were Bowleses, but the judge held firm. Having studied Miller's will for a month, he ruled Miller wanted the money to be given to his descendants "according to their roots, and not in equal shares."

This was only one of the trials of Sarah (Sally) Nickel Mein, who received only five million dollars from the estate instead of the nearly six million she had sought. First her son, William, ran off to marry Isolde, the family's German cook. She had barely recovered from her surprise when her other son, Tommy, married a Chinese-Pakistani woman named Farida Ismail who named their first son Twain Mein.

Sally Mein and her husband, William Wallace Mein, Jr., who, like his son, was always known as Tommy, lived in Woodside, a conservative, ultra-social village where there was little to talk about except the health of the horses or the surliness of the town smithy. Then, along came the Galvins.

John Galvin, a former Australian public-relations man, was an economic mover of the class of Huntington and Crocker. He bought up tin and iron mines abandoned by the Japanese in Malaya at the end of the war and quickly made an enormous fortune. Eager for social recognition, he moved his shy Irish wife and five children to California, bought an estate in Woodside, and filled the house with Oriental art treasures. To his surprise, he was snubbed by the Golden Circle. He kept trying. He founded the Los Altos Hunt Club and imported hunters and jumpers from Ireland (some costing twenty thousand dollars each) for his children and their friends to ride. He bought ranches in different parts of California and bought the two-hundred-thousand-dollar penthouse on Russian Hill that had once belonged to Templeton Crocker. Still, he was snubbed. Deciding to try an oblique attack, he moved to his ranch in Santa Barbara and vied for entrance to society there.

He finally got recognition, but not of the sort he wanted. The Internal Revenue Service investigated his enterprises and announced that he owed them twenty-two million dollars. Although this amount was reduced to twelve million and was paid by Galvin, he gave up on the United States and moved his family to an estate outside Dublin to live the undisturbed life of a country squire.

The disintegrating Golden Circle was horrified when Heidi McGurrin, a cotillion debutante educated at Foxcroft, an exclusive girl's school in Virginia, married a black jazz musician. She divorced him and married another black man. Sarah Foster Wylie, another young woman from an established family of the Golden Circle, was abruptly dropped from the Social Register when she married Hannibal Williams, a leader of San Francisco's black community.

The young and rich were quickly caught up in the drug scene. The girls insisted their parents hire the best of the rock bands to play at coming-out parties. A thoroughly stoned Grateful Dead played at the garden debut of sisters Lyn and Ayn Mattei. The W. Mackall Jasons hired the Beach Boys to play for their daughter's debut, but begged society editors not to mention it in advance for fear of crashers. The youngsters were not always enchanted with their idols. When Janis Joplin sang obscenities at a dance at the Burlingame Country Club, an incensed deb threw a drink in her face.

Dolly Fritz was the best known heiress in San Francisco. She was an only child and the buffer between her two quarreling parents. When her mother was in the process of getting a divorce from Fritz, he retaliated by making Dolly his sole heir. Fritz died in the middle of the divorce proceedings and Dolly's mother sued successfully to break the will and claim a share. Dolly still received an estate of ten million dollars, mainly in Nob Hill real estate. Her mother remarried a banker named Laurance Tharp and thereafter had little to do with Dolly.

When she was in eighth grade, Dolly received an allowance of two hundred dollars a month. As a senior at Miss Hamlin's School for Girls, she drove to school in her own white Jaguar. The *Examiner's* society column caustically commented on the contrast between the Jaguar and her schoolgirl dress, pointing out that she and her Jaguar were becoming regulars at theater openings and parties around town. At this, the school's headmistress insisted that Dolly become a boarder for the remainder of the school year; the Jaguar went back into the garage.

The cotillion committee pointedly overlooked Dolly, but the Mardi Gras committee, whose job was fund raising, did not. She was persuaded to run for queen, and since contributions counted as votes, she won easily. After her election she took a real interest in the charity for which the Mardi Gras was given, the Children's Hospital.

The press, which publicized Dolly as San Francisco's

most eligible young lady, was delighted when they saw her with a Spanish prince, Don Gonzalo of Bourbon, a cousin of the king of Spain. The two met at the Napa Valley Ranch of Jose and Celia Cebrian in the summer of 1959. The prince stayed to attend the opera opening with Dolly and their engagement was announced soon afterward.

Celia was one of those totally individual young women who come along perhaps once in a generation. Not crazy like Zelda, she was a lovely madcap who was married at eighteen to her cotillion partner Donald McNear. She bore him three children before moving on to the more exciting life she shared with Jose (Joe) Cebrian. Celia exercised her remarkable ability as a hostess at Joe's country estate. She delved a bit in witchcraft and always celebrated her birthday, October 31, with a Halloween party. She loved to mix people—lovers and ex-lovers—and watch the results. She was dramatic in everything she did, right to the end.

In the 1960s, the Cebrians took their children—they now had a son of their own—to live for a year in Rome. Celia met an English newspaperman and fell wildly in love. It was not requited and she returned to San Francisco. Joe followed. "I was brokenhearted," he said, "but we made up and it was the best time of our marriage." Celia suffered from headaches and insomnia and was taking an increasing amount of pills. Joe recalled, "It happened so suddenly. We had been out late and she woke up feeling lousy. I gave her an Alka-Seltzer and covered her with an extra blanket. Perhaps she took a Demerol for her headache; I don't know. All at once she went into a coma. I got her to the hospital, but she never awakened. She died five days later."

In 1970 Joe married Gretchen Kirsch, who was supposed to be dying from a rare blood disease. Miraculously, she recovered and the couple had a daughter Cairo and a son Christian. Gretchen was as beautiful as Celia, but darker and more exotic. She was fascinated by Egypt and liked to toy with the idea that she was the reincarnation of one of that country's legendary beauties. She made many trips to Egypt, and on her return from one in 1976, announced to Joe that their marriage was over.

Joe and Celia split with Dolly Fritz after her engagement to Prince Gonzalo was broken, and she hurriedly married a young man named Donald MacMasters, who was reputed to be with the American Embassy in Paris. To escape Dolly's mother and the press, the couple moved to Paris. They had two children, but the marriage was stormy and soon led to an even stormier Nevada divorce. MacMasters ignored the court's custody judgment and carried off the children. Later, the court forced him to return them.

Dolly's second marriage, to a Sacramento businessman named Newton Cope, was the first happy and stable time of her life. Cope adopted her two children and they had two more of their own. They lived quietly in their San Francisco apartment and at a country house in the Napa Valley. For the first time, Dolly was able to live away from the harsh light of publicity.

Since their social life was seldom publicized, the papers carried no story about the dinner party in their San Francisco apartment in February 1976. Guests remarked that Dolly never looked more radiant and beautiful. The following day, while taking an afternoon nap, she died in her sleep of a rare heart ailment. She was only forty.

Even in death, there was still trouble for the press's favorite "poor little rich girl." Donald MacMasters reappeared to file a six-hundred-fifty-thousand-dollar claim against her estate.

Phyllis Fraser, a tall blond with a shy smile and a breathy Marilyn Monroe voice, was the chief pilot of the jetset. Here, she was with an exiled Russian writer; there, she was with an Arabian oil sheik. She was off to Hollywood to travel somewhere on a chartered yacht, then she was back; she was being tutored by the heretical Episcopal bishop James Pike and she was off again. She didn't actually seem to live anywhere; she was always coming or going.

She was from someplace, though. Born and raised in a quiet, small town in Colorado, she finished high school and chose to go to the University of California at Berkeley. Suddenly, caught up in the tumultuous social world of the Bay Area, she met a wealthy contractor named Robert Fraser who fell in love with her and convinced her to marry him.

Fraser was madly in love with her beauty. He commissioned the Greek sculptor, Spero Anargyros, to make a bronze statue of her in the nude, which he placed in their living room. Unfortunately, beyond their agreement that she was a remarkably lovely woman, they had little in common. That was not enough to hold their marriage together. They divorced, and he provided her with a generous allowance for five years, even though it was quite likely she would marry again soon, probably to someone wealthier than he. The statue was returned to Spero Anargyros, who stood it in his studio.

Phyllis rented a flat on Spruce Street. With her particular charm, she drew fashionable young people, decorators, artists, actors and young socialites to her circle. The more people that came to each party, the more that heard about it the next week—and the more that jammed her next party. She was sought after by aspiring hostesses who wanted her name on their invitation lists, by newspaper columnists who wanted the latest gossip, and by husbands who complained that their wives didn't understand them. Each weekend the furniture was moved outside into the garden, tables were set up, food laid out, wine bottles uncorked, and a new party would begin.

She waited confidently for a new husband to appear. In the meantime, there was time for affairs. The society columns reported she was with Clay Callaway III, of the wealthy southern textile-manufacturing family. Callaway was the husband of Pia Lindstrom, the daughter of Ingrid Bergman and one of Phyllis's best friends. Her dinner for the newlywed Sterling Hayden and his New York socialite wife, Kitty, lasted until six in the morning and ended with a brawl in which Clay Callaway tumbled down the stairs. Then it was reported that it was over between Phyllis and Clay Callaway.

Next the papers connected her with Charles Spalding, a New York investment banker. This time, it was reported she would marry. Again there was a problem: his wife, the mother of his six children, stubbornly refused to recognize the divorce a Reno judge gave him.

Before she knew it, five years elapsed; her alimony ended, and there was no new husband. She was forced to sell her Lincoln convertible and some of her fur coats. She fell behind on the rent for her flat.

She approached one of her friends, Nancy Jackson, the blue-eyed, blond wife of a Beverly Hills attorney, for advice. Nancy listened attentively and then told Phyllis she had the solution to all her problems: transcendental meditation.

In 1964 transcendental meditation was not yet known to the Hollywood and rock-and-roll stars who would soon fly to the Maharishi Mahesh Yogi's air-conditioned meditation retreat in India. Nancy had to explain: all she had to do was sit a certain way, repeat a certain meaningless word, let her mind drift, and she would be in touch with the cosmic reality. That sounded fine to Phyllis, but she didn't understand how it would solve her problems. Once you were in touch with the cosmic reality, Nancy explained, it didn't matter if you had any problems.

Nancy explained enthusiastically that Phyllis didn't even have to go to India; she had invited the Maharishi to come to San Francisco. He was going to stay in a most improbable place, the home of Mrs. Frieda Klussmann on Telegraph Hill. This very conservative middle-aged society woman had, among other things, kept the city from getting rid of the cable cars in 1949. Nancy and Phyllis met Mrs. Klussmann on a trip to Russia. It was Nancy who talked her into letting the Maharishi use one of her many guest rooms and hold his services in her huge living room.

Nancy and her friends smiled happily. Mrs. Klussmann was polite when the Maharishi, a tiny brown-skinned man with a white Santa-Claus beard, flowing white robes, and an inane smile, was led into her living room. He greeted those present in a high, sing-song voice and scattered flowers on the carpet. His assistants had built a flower-covered throne in the middle of Mrs. Klussmann's living room and he took his place on it, neatly plopping himself into a lotus position. With considerable difficulty, Nancy and her friends copied this position. Sitting on the floor, they listened intently as he, with waving hands, described the pursuit of cosmic reality.

Phyllis claimed she was not feeling well, so she was not there the first night. On the second night, Nancy prevailed on her to come over, and she was given a private session with the Maharishi. Phyllis thanked Nancy afterward and went home.

Nancy did not hear from her the next day. Two days later, she called Phyllis. Phyllis explained that she was not feeling well, and had stayed home. Nancy was concerned about her being ill and alone in the Spruce Street flat. She consulted Mrs. Klussmann and asked Phyllis to come over and stay with them in the big red house until she was feeling better; there were plenty of bedrooms. Phyllis agreed and soon arrived carrying her overnight bag into the house which now smelled strongly of flowers and incense.

That night, while the Maharishi was instructing his pupils, Phyllis went to bed early. When the service was over, shortly after one in the morning, Nancy quietly opened the door and looked in on Phyllis. She wore a red nightgown and was asleep on the pink-blanketed bed. "Her breathing seemed awfully deep," Nancy recalled, "But then she turned on her side, and it sounded normal."

At eight the next morning, Nancy returned to the bedroom to wake Phyllis. "She was lying on her back. There was something in her posture. You got a feeling. . . . I touched her arm and it was cold."

She screamed for her husband. He rushed into the

room. While she tried to revive Phyllis, he called an ambulance. When, a few minutes later, the ambulance roared into the driveway of the big house, the neighbors assumed Mrs. Klussmann was dead. The woman next door put her head outside her window and called to the others gathered below. "I guess she's gone." The French maid overheard as she arrived for work. Sadly, she went upstairs to clean up Mrs. Klussmann's bedroom. She was terribly startled to find Mrs. Klussmann not only alive, but hurriedly getting dressed. It was going to be a long day.

Downstairs, a doctor arrived and pronounced Phyllis dead. As her body was carried out to the ambulance, a small crowd of friends and reporters began to gather next to the flower-covered throne in the living room. Suddenly, the Maharishi appeared. He had evidently been told the news. He waved away the reporters. Walking backwards toward the front door, he tossed flowers at them and lamented, in a high voice, "Too bad, too bad." Then he was gone.

The cause of Phyllis's death was acute bronchitis. Her parents were dead, but her brother and three sisters were notified. Charles Spalding flew to California for the funeral at Grace Cathedral.

The jetset was unaccustomed to funerals, but they did their best. Wrapped in furs, their cheeks streaked with mascara and tears, they listened to Bishop Pike read the service. "She was too sweet and vulnerable," one of them said sadly afterward. "She was her own worst enemy."

San Francisco had not seen the last of Charles Spalding. A close friend of the Kennedy brothers, he came to California in 1968, to work on Bobby Kennedy's primary campaign. In a whirlwind courtship, he met and won a lovely blond named Amy Ann Sullivan, a wealthy young widow from Hillsborough. They were married in St. Dominic's Catholic Church; Ted Kennedy was best man and the Kennedy in-laws, Stephen Smith and Peter Lawford, were in attendance.

Not long afterward, it was discovered that Spalding was relying on the Reno divorce that his wife, the mother of his six children, refused to recognize. Amy Ann was philosophic. The marriage, she said, was only bigamous in New York. Friends were glad to see her so happy. They knew she had terminal cancer.

Her brothers were less happy, but the scandal was kept under wraps. Not until after her death did the Internal Revenue Service come out with a ruling that the more than one million dollars she willed to Spalding was not properly a "husband's trust." He owed the government nearly half a million dollars in taxes because New York State refused to recognize his Nevada divorce.

Spalding went back to New York. However, he seemed to be infatuated with San Francisco and its women. He obtained a bona fide divorce and married Berenice Roth Grant, daughter of the William P. Roths and granddaughter of the shipping tycoon Captain William Matson.

Among the well-heeled newcomers to San Francisco was John Fell Stevenson, the son of Adlai Stevenson, twice the Democratic nominee for president and, in 1962, the ambassador to the United Nations. John was a handsome, rather shy young man, not long out of Harvard and ripe for romance. He fell in love with the twin daughters of Nathaniel Owings, the eminent architect.

Natalie and Emily Owings shared an apartment on Telegraph Hill where John visited frequently. To solve his dilemma, he chose Natalie.

Natalie Owings was one of the original flower children, a deceptively frail-looking brunette who was devoted to poetry, romance, nature, music, abstract painting and the pursuit of the elusive cosmic reality. As a couple, they resembled a college professor and a wood nymph, and seemed to have as much in common, but they were in fact engaged. In February, 1962, they planned to be married at the Owings home in Big Sur.

This was news to everyone, but especially to *Life* magazine, a picture magazine that specialized in wars, Marilyn Monroe, celebrities and picturesque, tree-surrounded houses. Since this wedding qualified on the last two counts, *Life* secured the exclusive right to photograph the ceremony.

This, needless to say, irked the social press of San Francisco, who felt they had just as much right to the wedding, if not more, than *Life* magazine. They made preparations to storm Big Sur (if necessary, by force) to get their pictures. Nathaniel Owings, who was as stubborn as the San Francisco press, made preparations to defend the wedding. Barricades were set up in the driveway and guards were planted in the trees.

At the last minute, either a war or Marilyn Monroe distracted *Life* magazine and they announced they would not cover the wedding after all. When the reporters, prepared to do battle for the right of the press to invade any ceremony, arrived at the barricades, their names were called on walkie-talkies to the house, and then, to their amazement, they were allowed in.

Walking into the strange house, the press immediately

spotted Adlai Stevenson in a tailcoat that touched his ankles, looking rather forlorn. The presence of John's mother, his former wife, Ellen Borden Stevenson, was the apparent cause of his discomfiture.

Mrs. Stevenson, wearing a black eye patch, was complaining to the reporters already present that she was not getting the attention she deserved. When she had married Adlai, she had been a leading Illinois society belle; he had been a quiet politician. The two of them got along like fire and wood. Even after they were divorced, and while he was governor of Illinois, she kept after him, holding press conferences to denounce him as a bad politician and a bad father. She even endorsed his opponents in elections.

While the press was diverted by Ambassador Stevenson and his wife, John and Natalie, oblivious to the circus around them, were married. The whole party moved along the coast to Nepenthe, a restaurant overlooking the ocean on a rocky site where Orson Welles had once lived in a cottage with Rita Hayworth. Natalie attacked the enormous wedding cake with such enthusiasm that it fell off the table. One of the photographers circled round the couple was barely able to catch it.

The couple moved into a large Victorian mansion in San Francisco, and decorated it with odd novelties, posters, giant pillows, and Natalie's artwork. Friends floated in and out, staying for an afternoon or a month, as was the custom in those loose and happy houses. But, somehow, for that couple, it didn't work. The son of Adlai Stevenson just didn't fit among giant pillows, strange paintings and scattered mattresses.

Natalie and John were divorced in 1971. Natalie stayed with her artist friends to continue her quest of the elusive cosmic reality. John married Elizabeth Flood, the great-granddaughter of James Flood, the Silver King.

In those chaotic years, you never knew what would happen next, and when it did happen, you weren't sure you believed it. Early in the morning of July 11, 1967, a police paddywagon brought a load of oddly garbed men and women to the door of the Parkside Police Station, between the Haight-Ashbury and the Golden Gate Park. A police officer led them inside and announced that they had been arrested for disturbing the peace and smoking marijuana. The desk sergeant began to book them.

He came to a sullen young man with long, mussed, brown hair, dressed in a red-lined, blue, double-breasted pea jacket, a brightly colored shirt and boots.

"Name?"

"Rudolf Nureyev," the young man said.

The desk sergeant wrote "Noureev."

The woman behind him was wrapped in a white mink stole.

"Name?"

"Margot Fonteyn."

The desk sergeant wrote it down. He asked her her age. She refused to answer. In a few minutes, all eighteen of them were jailed at the Hall of Justice. By dawn, the police realized whom they had jailed and calls were made to city hall. At seven-thirty A.M., V.H. Clark, the manager of the British Royal Ballet Company, arrived to bail out his dancers at $330 dollars each. He asked them what had happened.

After the performance of *Paradise Lost* at the Opera House, the dancers had gone to Trader Vic's for drinks and a late supper with an entourage of young admirers. They stayed until the restaurant closed. Then, one of their admirers suggested they go to the Haight-Ashbury to see what the hippies were doing. Nureyev and Fonteyn thought that was a fine idea.

As they drove through the nearly deserted streets of the Haight-Ashbury, they heard music and saw a party through the windows of an apartment at 42 Belvedere Street. Someone leaned out the window and invited them in, so they stopped, parked the car and went in.

At three thirty A.M., one of the neighbors called the police to complain about the noise. A single policeman knocked on the door of the apartment. When the door opened to the black uniform and badge, people panicked, yelled, pushed, and fled to the roof of the apartment house. The policeman pursued them with his flashlight. He found Nureyev lying flat on the gravel roof, and Dame Margot crouched on an adjacent roof with four young people.

16. THE TROJAN CHINCHILLA

The solemn gray San Francisco Opera House was the last fortress of the Golden Circle in their desperate battle to keep the jetset apart. Everyplace else had already fallen: the Mardi Gras, the Burlingame Country Club—even Hillsborough had been overrun.

The principal line of defense was the carriage entrance of the Opera House. Here, on opening night in the fall, a long, slow-moving line of black limousines deposited the gowned and white-tied members of society. They were greeted by a crowd of spectators and the society editors of the *Chronicle* and *Examiner*. The object of the defense was to keep those who were not from an old, Golden Circle family from being noticed on the society pages.

At the doorway of the opera, two photographers, one from the *Chronicle* and one from the *Examiner,* were positioned. With each photographer was a copy boy whose job was to rush up to those photographed to verify the name for the caption. Behind each photographer were the field captains of the defense, the society editors, who would select the subjects for the photographs.

Just inside the foyer of the Opera House was the second line of defense, the fashion editors. Each of these was also supported by a photographer and a copy boy. Their job was to select and photograph any strikingly new or fashionable attire that came through the door.

The commanding general of this defense was Charles de Young Thieriot, the publisher of the *Chronicle*. For the last several years, he had watched the rise of the jetset with dismay; his own society page was being filled with the names of people he did not know and parties to which he had not been invited.

He gave the order that no one was to be mentioned on the society page unless they were from an old family. He taped a roster of the Burlingame Country Club to the top of his desk to check the work of his editors.

At that year's opera opening, the society editor took Thieriot's command literally. The next day, the society page showed pictures of, not just the oldest names, but the oldest people at the opera. There were pictures of women who looked as if they should have died years before, shuffling grimly into the Opera House in old-fashioned gowns, laden with pounds of jewels. Thieriot was horrified. He ordered that, henceforth, no one over fifty-five years of age would be photographed.

But this was a mere skirmish compared to the opera opening of 1966. The White House announced that Lady Bird Johnson, the wife of the president of the United States, would attend. That meant the national press would be there, in addition to television crews from the networks and all the local stations. It also meant the jetset would assuredly be there in force, redoubling their effort to be noticed. Thieriot had already received an alarming bulletin that Valerie Naify, a jetset leader, former model and the wife of theater-chain tycoon Marshall Naify, had ordered a thirty-thousand-dollar black and blue Rolls-Royce and was expecting delivery right before the opera opening.

Preparations for the battle began days before the September 20 opening. Hairpieces and gowns were ordered, rented limousines were contracted for, appointments were made with hairdressers, and arrangements were made for strongboxes of family jewels to be taken from bank safe-deposit boxes. Reservations for preopera and postopera suppers had been made long before.

On the day of the opening, Secret Service agents prowled the Opera House, looking behind curtains and poking under the seats. The drinking fountains were checked for acid or corrosives concealed in the faucets. The manhole covers outside the Opera House were sealed. All trash cans and restrooms were checked for explosives. Unmarked government cars filled with communications equipment and automatic weapons were parked unobtrusively outside the Opera House. Late in the afternoon, security guards stationed at the stage door confirmed that the members of the chorus were actually members of the chorus. Shortly afterwards, it was confirmed that Joan Sutherland was Joan Sutherland.

By seven-thirty, a crowd of several hundred people had gathered behind the police barricades. A number of them came to demonstrate against the Vietnam War. They began chanting: "Hey, Hey, L.B.J., how many boys did you kill today?"

Grim-faced Secret Service agents, holding walkie-talkies, watched them from inside the foyer. Soon they were joined by the society editors and cameramen (loaded down with lenses and equipment cases) who came from a preopera supper a hundred yards away at the Museum of Art. As the crowd became larger and noisier, television lights snapped on and bathed the carriage entrance in a harsh white glare. The demonstrators, seeing the lights and TV cameras, began chanting louder. Kurt Herbert Adler, the stout, white-haired director of the opera, and a sleek white-tied Robert Watt Miller, president of the Opera Association and a defender of the old guard, took their places between the Secret Service and the society editors. Wearing broad smiles, they prepared to meet Mrs. Johnson.

The first limousines began arriving at the carriage entrance, while three hundred people walked across the courtyard from the supper at the Museum of Art; the battle was about to begin. Blazes of white light from cameramen's flashguns lit the carriage entrance as reporters called out, "Get her!" and "Get that man with the opera hat!" The demonstrators, not knowing what was going on, began chanting louder. Then, a gleaming black and blue Rolls-Royce shouldered its way to the curb. Editors told their photographers to ignore it; the jetset was arriving.

The door of the Rolls-Royce opened and Mrs. Naify stepped out, wearing an ankle-length mink coat. That was the strategy of the jetset: they knew they had little chance of getting the attention of the society editors, but, if they were extravagant enough in their furs, the fashion editors inside the door couldn't possibly ignore them. After her, came Mrs. Emil Magliocco in a full-length chinchilla. Mrs. Louis Hirshhorn, accompanied

242

not by her husband but (more appropriately) by her furrier, wore a nine-thousand-dollar black sable. Then, outshining them all, came Joan Hitchcock wrapped in a full-length sable coat that cost her husband thirty-five thousand dollars.

Mmes. Magliocco, Naify, Hirshhorn and Hitchcock smiled and walked by the society editors, who stonily ignored them. It was not unheard of for a member of the jetset to ask a society editor to take her picture; the society editor would reply, icily, "I'm sorry, we're busy." One jetsetter even hired her own photographer to take her picture as she arrived, hoping to deceive the society editors, but they saw through her ruse and ignored her. The brilliantly-furred jetsetters feigned indifference to the society writers; they waited for the fashion editors to see them.

The crush at the carriage entrance was unbelievable. The demonstrators were chanting louder than ever, the people on the outside of the doors were pushing forward to see what was going on inside, and the people on the inside of the foyer were pushing out to see what all the commotion was outside. In the middle of the crush, Adler and Miller were still smiling broadly, waiting for Mrs. Johnson.

Meanwhile, Mrs. Johnson, wearing a gold-brocade gown, was in her box inside, smiling and waiting impatiently for Miller and Adler. Fearing the phalanx of demonstrators outside, the Secret Service escorted her into the Opera House through the taxi entrance, on the opposite side of the building from the carriage entrance. As part of their program of total security, they notified no one.

As the last guests arrived, it occurred to Miller and

Adler that they were in the wrong place. They hurried upstairs toward Miller's box, fighting the crowd on their way to the bar to avoid the intermission crush after the first act.

Two photographers from the *Chronicle* and the *Examiner,* stationed outside Miller's box, saw Mrs. Johnson first. Just as Miller arrived, they took her picture, and the door to the box was rudely slammed by the Secret Service. Miller convinced the Secret Service and Mrs. Johnson's press secretary of his identity and the door opened once more to admit him. He was introduced to the First Lady, they took their seats, the lights dimmed, and the opera began.

From the orchestra, the balconies and the other boxes, the audience looked around to see Mrs. Johnson and the Secret Service agents. The probable cost of Joan Hitchcock's sable coat was argued over Joan Sutherland's liquid voice singing *I Puritani.*

In Miller's box, a second intrigue was unwinding. Sometime during the first act, Mrs. Johnson discovered that Miller was not a Democrat; not only was he not a Democrat, he was a hard-core, devoted, life-long Republican. Normally this would not have made a difference, but 1966 was an election year. Sitting in the box with the presidential party was the wife of Governor Edmund G. Brown, a Democrat running for reelection against Ronald Reagan. Mrs. Brown and the First Lady wanted to persuade some of the wealthy Democrats at the opera to give money to Brown's campaign. Mrs. Johnson learned that Louis Petri, a prominent California wine millionaire and a Democrat, was in an adjoining box. The First Lady and Mrs. Brown indicated their wish to see Petri at the intermission.

Joan Sutherland disappeared from the stage. The stalwarts at the bar looked at their watches and grumbled that their reverie was about to be disturbed by intermission. Mrs. Johnson, smiling, left her box to find and overwhelm Mr. Petri. Suddenly, she found Miller's elbow linked in hers and the chairman of the County Republican Fund Raising Committee, Milton Esberg, rapidly approaching from the other side. Miller, sensing her plot and being a good Republican, saw his chance to help Ronald Reagan and revenge his being left in the foyer. Miller and Esberg steered the hapless First Lady through the lobby behind the boxes, keeping her ten yards from any wealthy Democrats. When the intermission ended, she had not come close to Louis Petri.

Miller and Esberg steered her back to Miller's box; Mrs. Johnson thanked them and sat down. Miller smiled happily, thinking Mrs. Johnson would now be unable to move until the opera was over. Mrs. Johnson thought otherwise.

Determined to get at Petri's wallet, Mrs. Johnson whispered to the Secret Service agent behind her. Accompanied by her press secretary and the Secret Service, Mrs. Johnson stood up, smiled apologetically at Miller and tiptoed down the hall to Mr. Petri's box.

Mrs. Johnson was still having difficulty. Mr. Petri was not in his box; he was with the stalwarts at the bar, happily drinking. A Secret Service agent was dispatched to tell him the wife of the president of the United States was waiting for him.

By the time Mrs. Johnson got hold of Petri, Mmes. Hitchcock, Naify and Magliocco were planning their departure and members of the audience were taking final bets on the value of Mrs. Hitchcock's sable coat. At the bar, the stalwarts downed their last drink and discussed where they would adjourn to. Someone noticed the opera had ended and Joan Sutherland standing expectantly on the stage; they began clapping. Soon the whole audience was cheering and applauding that the opera was over.

Turmoil began again as the audience poured from the theatre; the few remaining demonstrators resumed their chant, Mrs. Naify's black-and-blue Rolls-Royce reappeared and Mrs. Johnson was rushed down the back stairs and sped away in a black limousine. As one of the old guard, Mrs. G. Willard Somers of Woodside, said, "It was a shattering evening. We aren't used to that."

Mrs. Johnson's efforts were for naught; Ronald Reagan defeated Governor Brown six weeks later. The jetset's efforts were rewarded. *Chronicle* society pages carried no pictures of Mrs. Naify's black and blue Rolls-Royce, nor of Mrs. Hitchcock's thirty-five-thousand-dollar sable nor of Mrs. Hirshhorn in her nine-thousand-dollar sable, but, there in all her glory, wrapped from neck to ankle in chinchilla, was Mrs. Emil Magliocco. The fashion editors had been unable to resist; another fortress had fallen. Now, even the opera opening belonged to the jetset.

17. BUMP AND HUSTLE

In August 1968 the city's irascible philanthropist Alma deBretteville Spreckels died; she was eighty-seven. Since her coffin was so enormous it would not fit through the door of the sugar cake mansion, her funeral was held at the Palace of the Legion of Honor. A mass of relatives stood near the coffin.

One would not have thought Alma would have found time for romance, but she had. After Adolph died, she was alone for years. Then, in 1939, she eloped in a private plane with Elmer Awl, a rancher from Santa Barbara.

They were, to say the least, a picturesque couple. Arriving at the opera, Alma was the warrior queen, tall, imposing, head high; she was regal from her elaborate coiffure to her bedroom slippers. Awl, as if he played the part of Gary Cooper, wore a neatly-brushed stetson and mirror-shined cowboy boots.

Unfortunately, the marriage lasted only four years. Its downfall, it was said, came when Alma was entertaining the extremely urbane and reserved English author Somerset Maugham. As usual, the conversation in Alma's parlor was conducted largely in French, which she preferred. At a particularly elevated point in the conversation, Awl arrived with his drinking companions, whom he showed into the room. Alma's glare probably could have killed the houseplants.

Awl left, and Alma took her companionship from her family. She had a son, Adolph, Jr., and two daughters, Dorothy and Alma. Alma was referred to as "Little Alma" or "Alma Junior" to distinguish her from her mother who was very aptly called "Big Alma." Adolph, Jr., inherited some of the traits of the Spreckels family; he was independent and stubborn which led to titanic arguments with his mother. He left home as soon as he could and started the first of what turned out to be seven marriages—none of them peaceful. The last and most notable, as far as the gossip columnists were concerned, was to Kay Williams, who divorced him to marry Clark Gable.

The daughters were more like Alma probably than even Alma liked. Both of them, who were also great arguers, left home early for ultimately unhappy and short-lived marriages. They were soon back at the white sugar cake mansion and then off again with new husbands. Like their mother, they couldn't do anything in an ordinary way.

Little Alma married John Rosekrans, a handsome gentleman who was the father of her three sons. Then, she married James Coleman, a descendant of William O'Brien, the Silver King. Next, to the surprise of no one who knew the Spreckelses, she married Charles Hammel, the captain of a freighter.

She and Hammel set off, alone, on a forty-foot sloop, with a full load of frozen food, announcing they were sailing to Hawaii. Alma knew nothing about sailing; Hammel was less knowledgeable than might be expected of an old-time seafaring man. They did not arrive on the day scheduled, or the following day, or the day after that. Finally, the Coast Guard sent planes and cutters to search for them. They found nothing. The sloop had vanished. The search was called off, and the Spreckels family prepared to go into mourning.

Then the sloop appeared in Hawaii, with Alma and Hammel safe aboard, but much the worse for the voyage. The boat's electrical system had been knocked out. Alma, it seemed, always had to do things the hard way. They returned hastily by plane to San Francisco and were divorced not long afterward. Alma took back her maiden name, Spreckels, and the captain vanished from the Social Register.

Dorothy's third husband was a Palm Beach man named Charles Munn; he was considerably older than she and even richer. In the winter they lived in his house, called Amado, in Palm Beach. In the spring, they flew to Paris and stayed in an apartment they kept there. In the summer they came back to San Francisco. Occasionally, their routine was broken. One spring, it rained continually in Paris; Munn was miserable and laid up in bed. Dorothy told him he should go back to Palm Beach, where at least the sun was shining. She called the airlines and asked about flights from Paris to Palm Beach. There were none.

A day later, a Boeing 727 touched down at Palm

Beach airport and rolled to a stop at the terminal. A ramp was wheeled to the plane and two passengers, Dorothy and Charles Munn, stepped out. Munn was driven to Amado and Dorothy had the plane returned.

Little Alma lived in a modern Pacific Heights mansion whose interior was done entirely in stark black and white. Dorothy, in the sun room of her mansion, reclined in an antique chair. A writer visiting her in Palm Beach marveled at the furniture; springs poked through the seats of chairs and cushions creaked. Where else would such springs and sagging cushions be acceptable, he wondered. In the sun room of the sugar cake mansion, the chairs were covered by peculiar little doilies. "Isn't it marvelous," Dorothy said, "to be rich enough to be tacky?"

The younger children of the Golden Circle sometimes went to odd extremes to amuse themselves. On a warm summer night in August 1969, San Francisco society was horrified to learn that one of the victims of the Manson murders in the Bel-Air mansion of Sharon Tate was Abigail Folger of the coffee clan. Radcliffe-educated and beautiful, no one in San Francisco suspected Abigail had connection with the Hollywood drug culture.

They were no less startled when Frederick Newhall Woods III, a twenty-four-year-old descendant of the Newhall family of Woodside, and two of his friends from Atherton were arrested in July 1976, after they allegedly kidnapped an entire school bus full of children outside the town of Chowchilla and hid them in a buried moving van.

On a brisk afternoon in the autumn of 1975, two men in business suits climbed the back stairs of a run-down house in San Francisco's Outer Mission district. As they neared the top of the stairs, a young woman's face appeared in the window of the door.

"FBI and police, freeze!" the first man shouted, pointing a gun at her. The two men pushed through the door. The FBI agent kept his gun pointed at the young woman and the police inspector rushed after a second woman who was fleeing toward a back room. "Hold it. Turn around," he ordered. The young woman stopped and turned around. "Aren't you glad it's over?" the police inspector asked. Patricia Campbell Hearst looked at him blankly. He handcuffed her and led her down the stairs to a waiting police car.

By that time, there was hardly anyone in the world who didn't know that she, the granddaughter of William Randolph Hearst, had been abducted from her apartment in Berkeley by a strange revolutionary group called the Symbionese Liberation Army and that, after a few weeks, she announced she had joined her kidnappers. The press reported every imaginable detail of the story— from what she wore when she was kidnapped to the fact that the Timex watch on the wrist of the body of the leader of the SLA was still running after the Los Angeles shootout.

Reporters camped outside her parents' mansion in Hillsborough hoping for a story. They crushed into the courtroom in February 1976 when she was brought to trial. They explored newspaper files and talked to her friends to find out more about her and the society to which she belonged.

They found out what most people already knew: that she was the third of five daughters of Randolph Hearst, the publisher of the San Francisco *Examiner;* that, despite her parent's wishes, she had stopped going to

Mass; that she had been asked to leave the Santa Catalina School for Girls in Monterey (reportedly because she had been caught smoking marijuana) and enrolled, instead, in Crystal Springs, a private school near her home in Hillsborough. There, a University of California graduate student, Steven Weed, tutored her. She decided to go to college in Berkeley and moved into an apartment with Weed where she was living when she was kidnapped.

They learned that her best friend, Tricia Tobin, was the daughter of the president of the Hibernia Bank—the bank she had robbed—and the great-granddaughter of Michael de Young, the founder of the San Francisco *Chronicle*. They learned that the jail in Pleasanton where she was ordered to serve part of her sentence was six miles from the site of Hacienda del Pozo de Verona where her great-grandmother entertained guests under a painted Egyptian sky. But when reporters tried to learn more about San Francisco society, they had difficulties.

In Hillsborough, the exclusive suburb south of San Francisco, the rambling mansions that looked like Italian palaces and English castles and the modern glass houses were protected by electric gates and private security guards. Guards watched the gate of the Burlingame Country Club. The list of debutantes who would come out that year at the Cotillion was not public information. Neither were the names of boxholders at the San Francisco Opera.

Downtown, reporters trying to talk to the leaders of society found armed guards in the lobbies of the office buildings. There were guards by the elevators in the offices of the *Examiner* and the *Chronicle,* as well as at the private clubs. No one wanted to be seen or known;

society had gone into hiding. Children were sent to school under assumed names. Families refused to let the newspapers print engagement and wedding announcements. Telephone numbers were taken out of the phone book and bodyguards were hired to ride in the limousines.

What had happened to the families that had built the Italian palaces and the English castles in Hillsborough, and whose portraits hung in the museums they had built?

By the end of the sixties, the battle was over. Both sides wore themselves out. One of the jetset lamented, "We're all dead, divorced, or broke." The remaining members of the Golden Circle retreated to their hideaways.

The rituals of society continued, but they seemed empty—almost mockeries of themselves. The opera opening each September was still the major event on the calendar, but it looked different. As if there were not enough security guards hired by the Golden Circle, more were hired by the insurance companies who held policies on the jewelry. Eventually, it seemed simpler to leave the jewels in bank vaults; each year there was less glitter at the opera opening than the year before. Even more devastating was the fact that more and more people were going to the opera for no other reason than to hear the opera. If you couldn't talk with friends during *Aida,* what was the point of going to the opera in the first place?

The February Mardi Gras, which had once been a stellar evening of the prewar social season, got out of hand. Since the Queen of the Mardi Gras was elected by votes pledged to her name at ten cents a vote, this position was easily seized by the jetset. Mrs. Robert Naify, the sister-in-law of the owner of the celebrated black-and-blue Rolls-Royce, was elected queen in the late fifties. Milton Shoong, Jr., a member of a wealthy Chinese family, put up twenty thousand dollars on behalf of his blond Caucasian wife. She was elected, served as queen, and then divorced him. When Suzanne Bercut was elected queen in 1962, Terrence Malarkey, who had contributed a four-thousand-dollar check to elect his own wife, announced that he would not honor his check. Angrily, he claimed the Bercut money had come in after the deadline. The publicity that resulted forced him to honor the check, but an elaborate system of electronic vote tabulation was set up to prevent future controversies of that sort.

The Black and White Symphony Ball, a San Francisco invention widely copied by other cities, disappeared. It involved dancing to four different music tempos—waltz, Latin American, the fox trot, jazz (and later rock)—at four separate hotels. Women were expected to wear either black or white evening gowns or a combination of these colors. Hundreds of Symphony Association workers slaved for months on the decorations at the hotels, each group trying to outdo the others.

The Ball was dropped for a couple of years, then revived—with a difference. It was truly black and white. Members of the black community, educators Nathan Hare and his wife, Julia, and the Reverend Cecil Williams of Glide Memorial Church and his wife, Evelyn, got together with white friends and suggested the ball live up to its name. The blacks, however, were far outnumbered by the whites. Some said it was just token representation. In any case, the resulting publicity did

254

not help the city's racial problems. Neither did the performance of the Grateful Dead at the Hilton, when they brought along their entourage of pot-smokers and sullenly left after playing only a couple of sets. The Symphony Association looked to other ways to raise money for its ever-present deficit.

In 1941 Greenway's cotillions were revived by Millie Robbins (society editor of the *Chronicle),* Stuart Nixon (a protégé of Greenway's and assistant manager of the Palace Hotel) and Mrs. Nion Tucker, the former Phyllis de Young. They stopped almost immediately during the war, but began again afterward as a way to introduce debutantes to society. Percy King, grandson of the murdered editor James King of William, presented the girls and led the Cotillion marches he had learned from Greenway.

Much of Greenway's ritual was revived intact. The dancers promenaded and wheeled, formed arches and marched about the ballroom like a drill team. When King was in his nineties, he retired. Stuart Nixon and Warren Howell, a book dealer, took over. They announced the name of each young lady and she appeared in a white gown on the decorated stage of the Palace Ballroom.

Of all the defenders of the inner bastions of San Francisco society, Mrs. Tucker was the shrewdest. She saw the Mardi Gras fall to the jetset because they could buy the title of queen; she saw the opera fall, despite the efforts of her nephew Charles de Young Thieriot, because no one could match the jetset's chinchilla coats.

Although nearly every debutante ball around the country raised a huge amount of money for charity, the San Francisco Cotillion barely met expenses with the fees charged each debutante. Guests paid nothing for the coveted invitation. Mrs. Tucker turned this to a stroke of genius. As long as the Cotillion was not a charity fundraiser, they would not feel compelled to invite people because they had money. The Cotillion could be safely locked within the Golden Circle.

Thus, year after year, everyone at the Cotillion knew everyone else; it was a private party. Guests had all gone to grade school together and seen one another when they came home from boarding school. After the Cotillion, they all went skiing together in the mountains.

"We keep a low profile," Nixon said, "see the same friends and entertain back and forth. I don't know many of the people mentioned today on the society pages. It's not like the old days when life was simpler and you knew everyone."

Unable to penetrate Mrs. Tucker's simple but effective defenses, the outsiders set up rival cotillions. First there was a ball in the East Bay, called the Winter Ball, which benefited a children's hospital.

Next, the families that had come to the Peninsula after the war established their own ball, the Peninsula Ball, so they could bring out their children. Y.A. Tittle, the former quarterback of the New York Giants who sold insurance in the Bay Area, paid one thousand dollars and had the pleasure of seeing his daughter introduced. Although Charles Black came from a very respected and established family, he had made, by Social Register standards, the serious error of marrying a former movie actress. Shirley Temple was certainly not Marion Davies, but her name was not in the Register. The Blacks' older daughter was overlooked by the Cotillion and she came out at the Peninsula Ball.

Marin County, to the north of San Francisco, was the home of many of the newly wealthy people of the Bay Area. They preferred its rustic atmosphere, open hills and tree-filled valleys. Despite these advantages, they felt slighted that they did not have a debutante ball. A Marin Ball was established which would benefit an all-purpose organization called the Marin Charity Foundation. It cost seven hundred dollars per debutante.

The black community of San Francisco came next. They established the Linx Ball. Finally, a rival to the Cotillion sprang up in San Francisco itself. Called the San Francisco Debutante Ball, this affair charged one thousand dollars a debutante for the Presbyterian Hospital. Girls, not only from the newly wealthy families of San Francisco, but from as far away as Monterey and Stockton, were introduced.

But all these balls were victims of a cruel turn in fashion. In the seventies, it was all right to be wealthy, but it was increasingly unfashionable to let on that you were—especially if you were young. A reverse fashion code went into effect; the more money you had, the less money you were supposed to spend on clothes. The fashion at expensive private colleges was to dress like a romantic vision of a factory worker—in overalls, battered boots and kerchiefs—regardless of whether you were a man or a woman. Since real factory workers tried to dress as if they had money, this made the college student's costume even more striking. To wear anything but faded Levi's at Berkeley or Stanford was to invite the sort of disdain once reserved for those who did not wear a blazer and school tie or saddle shoes or a white blouse with a Peter Pan collar. Women, according to this fascinating new code, were to talk like longshoremen, frizz their hair, and go without underwear. Men were supposed to look like Hebrew prophets, young Russian revolutionaries or members of motorcycle gangs. The supreme, most vehemently, terribly wrong thing one could possibly do was to be seen in a white gown—unless one was barefoot at a wedding on a mountain in Big Sur with daisies in one's hair. In fact, the only thing worse than being seen in a white gown was to be seen in a white gown going to a debutante ball.

Thus, while the adults loved debutante balls, the debutantes themselves often considered them, at best, a mortal embarrassment and, at worst, a callous extravagance on a par with the exploitation of farmworkers and the war in Indochina. So few young women wanted to make debuts in Marin that the ball had to be canceled. In San Francisco, the organizers of the San Francisco Debutante Ball were forced to drop "Debutante" from the title; the young women were referred to as "honored guests." But even this was unsuccessful. In 1972 only seven "honored guests" could be found, so the San Francisco Ball quietly folded.

Even the Cotillion was beset by doubt. A young lady from a select family of the Golden Circle whose debut had long been awaited refused to come out. Her name was Patricia Hearst. Her grandfather, who had had his own problems with San Francisco society, might have understood.

The old kingdom of Hillsborough was scarcely recognizable. Sky Farm, once the pleasant seat of William W. Crocker (William H's son), had been purchased by Norman Stone, the son of a Chicago insurance millionaire, W. Clement Stone, who converted it to Nueva School, a private day school for gifted children. The collection of antique silver and French Impressionist paintings which once had a private curator were gone, and the walls of the forty rooms were tacked with children's drawings. A yellow school bus was parked in the driveway where the Rolls-Royces had been. Slides, swings and other playground equipment stood on the lawn. The white-pillared drawing room, arranged austerely with desks and filing cabinets, was the office. The huge kitchen was the art and science department. In the dining room, a long bar bolted to the wall was being used by young ballet students.

The Crocker empire had been purchased by the food-processing conglomerate of Foremost-McKesson, who sold only the house and immediate grounds to Stone. The land around it was being subdivided into lots of one-and-a-half acres and larger; new houses with Spanish tile roofs and French windows clustered around the mansion like a village around a castle.

The eighteenth-century Georgian manor of the Camerons, Rosecourt, was torn apart by 1973. It was purchased by James Kazan, the owner of a janitorial and building supplies firm, and Allan Sebanc, an elementary school principal. Sebanc was busy tearing down the kitchen and converting the dining room into a modern kitchen and family room which he planned to occupy. Kazan was building an Oriental-modern house right next to it. The music room was being pried off the house and added to a new house being built by attorney Kenneth McCloskey, Sebanc's brother-in-law. The swimming pool behind the house was being taken by Phil Lehr, the owner of a chain of steak houses, who was building a house next to it. The remaining seven and a half acres had been divided into eleven lots and they were being sold to Kazan and Sebanc's friends. The one hundred trees that surrounded the house were being sawed down to make room for the new village, which Kazan proudly announced would keep the name "Rosecourt."

Only six acres of grounds remained outside the great windy Parisian bus station Carolands. The house stood vacant until 1950, when it was bought by a cheerful, eccentric woman named Countess Lillian Dandini. She was the heiress to a local brick works fortune. Despite the fact that her count left her not long after her marriage, she carried on in a regal fashion in the ninety-two rooms of the mansion—ignoring the clouds of ashes, the banging of the windows and the noisy gurgling of the plumbing.

When she died in 1970, she generously left the mansion to the city of Hillsborough. The voters of Hillsborough took a look at it and refused to accept it. It went back on the real estate market and finally passed into the hands of a Canadian divorcée.

La Dolphine, the Hillsborough Petit Trianon, was bought by an eccentric woman who drove a half-ton truck. It had been considered a jinx by a series of owners starting with the George Newhalls, who built it in 1915. Dorothy Spreckels lived there during her second and unhappy marriage; the Richard Rheems lost their money while in residence there and the Hugh Chisholms never gave the parties they'd planned because Rosie Chisholm, a stepdaughter of William K. Vanderbilt, was desperately ill most of the time she lived there.

An inventor, Barrie Regan, and his wife bought the Charles Blyth estate, Strawberry Hill, but had no butler to run it. The Blyths' large staff was headed by a butler, also named Blyth. Few butlers remain in Hillsborough.

Angelo, who has been with the Christian de Guignes III since they were married, is an exception. Mr. de Guigne, a descendant of the French branch of the Parrott family, heads the Stauffer Chemical Company and has always had a butler. His Hillsborough neighbor, Bing Crosby, is less accustomed to this kind of help, but the actor-singer and his wife, Kathryn, find it handy to have Alan Fisher, their English butler, make most of their decisions about how to act in their roles as San Francisco socialites. When Fisher is in doubt, he calls "Aunt Phyllis," as all the Crosbys call Mrs. Nion Tucker.

Kathy Crosby is more than Bing's wife and the mother of their three children. She has a nursing degree and treats Mexican children when they stay at their place in La Paz. When the children were younger, she was a substitute teacher at their school in Hillsborough. In the 1970's, she started a daily television program.

The area's only other resident celebrity, Shirley Temple Black, is equally busy. After being blackballed by the Palo Alto Junior League, she finally became one of the group's most outstanding members. Then, she ran for Congress against Paul N. (Pete) McCloskey, whose wife, Cubby, was also in the Palo Alto League. This split the organization, but Cubby and her husband won. After that victory, they got a divorce. Shirley, secure in her marriage, went on to become the Republican party's highest money-maker at luncheon and dinner speeches.

Shirley was rewarded, first with a position in the United Nations, then, as ambassador to Ghana. Under President Ford, she was given the rank of chief of protocol.

Celebrity status of sorts can be claimed by others in San Francisco. Prentis Cobb Hale and his second wife,

Denise, formerly married to Vincente Minnelli, the Hollywood movie director, are always in the thick of international society. Actress Ina Claire Wallace, widow of William R. Wallace, the attorney, lives more quietly than she used to when Cecil Beaton, Noel Coward and the Duke and Duchess of Windsor came visiting.

On the go constantly are architect John Carl Warnecke, who has offices in New York and Washington. His wife, Grace, is the daughter of George Kennan, one-time ambassador to Russia. Grace speaks fluent Russian and frequently acts as interpreter for VIP visitors to America. The Warneckes' friends, Lita and Jack Vietor, are more likely to be flying to the Orient. Jack, a former publisher of *San Francisco Magazine,* is honorary consul to Nepal. He is also an international backgammon champion who participates in tournaments all over the globe. During the summer, when he and his attractive brunette wife are at home in La Jolla, he stages his own tournaments.

After William Sharon's death, William Ralston's magnificent Belmont mansion, with its silver balustrades and oval ballroom, was turned into a girl's seminary. Shortly afterward it became a mental hospital and it was that for twenty years. Then, for many years, it was empty.

In 1922 the Sisters of Notre Dame de Namur bought the house. The dust was swept out, the walls painted, the silver·polished, and it reopened as a college. The sisters proudly took visitors through the oval ballroom, showing them the chandeliers and mirrors that once reflected all of San Francisco society.

Ralston's gaudy Palace Hotel belonged to the Sharon family until 1954. That year, it was bought by the Sheraton Hotel chain and became the Sheraton-Palace. The Sheraton chain was purchased by International

Telephone and Telegraph. Then, in 1973, the hotel was bought by Kyo-Ya, a Japanese corporation, which was owned by Kokusai Kogyo, an even larger Japanese corporation. The Cotillion stayed on and crowds of Japanese tourists looked curiously at the few white-gowned debutantes walking self-consciously to the Grand Ballroom.

The noisy outside world had even invaded the tree-shaded sanctuary of Pacific Heights. For years, the diplomatic community had chosen to live here. Consulates, with their flagpoles and bronze plaques, were found on every street.

The arrival of the consulates was followed by the arrival of the demonstrators, then, terrorists. The windows of Pacific Heights mansions were periodically rattled by bombs exploding. In January 1967, a bomb blew up the Yugoslavian consulate on Pacific Avenue. Iranian students continually picketed the Iranian consulate on Washington Street; one student set himself on fire on the sidewalk in front of the house. Finally in October 1971, dynamite demolished the house. In 1976 a bomb wrecked the South African consulate.

If that was not bad enough, residents of Pacific Heights learned that one of their neighbors was assembling a military arsenal in his own basement. In April 1967 a dozen federal agents raided the home of William E. Thoresen III at 2801 Broadway, a charming mansion with a pair of curving steps leading to a doorway flanked by Corinthian columns. In the basement, they found rifles, pistols, dynamite, machine guns, flame throwers, and antitank guns. Thoresen mildly explained that he liked to collect things and there had been a lot of burglaries in the neighborhood lately.

When the Russians opened a consulate in San Francisco in 1971, they announced that their consul-general, Alexander Zinchuk, wanted to live in Pacific Heights. The neighbors welcomed the idea as warmly as they would an announcement that a leper colony or a houseful of drug addicts was moving in.

Fortunately for the Russians, Zinchuk, a slight, mild-looking man with brown hair and clear blue eyes, had considerable charm. It was also rumored that he was a spy, and there was something romantic about the idea of a Russian spy living next door. After lengthy and acrimonious negotiations, the Russians got Zinchuk a house in the same Broadway block as the Thoresen mansion. Among the neighbors were: the Gordon Gettys, Dodie and John Rosekrans, Joe Cebrian and the Roman Catholic archbishop, Joseph McGucken. The Russians had no need to worry that Thoresen would turn his antitank guns on them if their parties were too noisy; his wife had murdered him the year before.

Zinchuk invited the neighborhood to a house warming. Nearly all accepted. They found the mansion girded by a high wrought-iron fence. Inside, Zinchuk and his wife received their guests. Tables were set with vodka and caviar in rooms painted a sunny yellow. Chairs upholstered in cut gold velvet and brocade surrounded a teak dining table from Gump's that seated fourteen. "No Chinese influence," announced the decorator.

Then, in March 1973 a houseful of drug addicts announced they were moving in. They were not ordinary drug addicts; they were members of a self-help organization called Delancey Street. John Maher, a cheery man with a modest bush of brown hair who wore conservative dark three-piece suits that made him look like a progressive banker or an advertising executive, headed the group. He had once been a drug addict on New York's Lower East Side. With the aid of a self-help group called Synanon, he kicked his own habit and organized Delancey Street to give addicts and ex-convicts counseling, jobs and, most of all, a sense of family. Soon they were running a moving business, a flower shop, and a garden restaurant on Union Street, all staffed by ex-addicts who adopted a life of strict discipline and were fiercely devoted to their new "family."

When they needed a headquarters, they bought a square twenty-five-room white mansion at the corner of Divisadero and Broadway Streets, in the center of Pacific Heights for one hundred and sixty-five thousand dollars. Immediately, the neighbors were outraged. When Maher applied to have his foundation legally considered a "family" to comply with the zoning laws, the neighbors packed the hearing room of the Board of Permit Appeals to protest.

One woman, who lived next door to the mansion complained that she heard hammering sounds from the mansion late at night. "You simply don't hammer after midnight in a nice neighborhood," she said. Neighbor after neighbor stood up to defend what Delancey Street was doing, but not in Pacific Heights. Others, who had been neighbors of Delancey Street's previous headquarters, disagreed violently. "They're good neighbors," one woman protested. "They made the house into a warm, friendly place."

Finally, Maher himself stood up to speak. Dozens of members of his "family" stood in the back of the hearing room. He was dressed in one of his three-piece suits and smiled at his friends in the audience. "Pacific Heights," he said, "is a very beautiful and isolated area where some people have forgotten that social problems in the community don't only have to be solved in the Fillmore." The Planning Commission rejected his application, but, after lengthy appeals, Maher finally won and his "family" moved into the white mansion.

In August 1975 a motion picture crew was intently at work in the bedroom of Joan Hitchcock's mansion on Broadway. The star of the film, a young lady named Amber Hunt, was in a rather indelicate position on Joan Hitchcock's bed.

"Okay, Amber, give me a little more ass," the director urged. They were filming something entitled *Cry for Cindy,* which was scheduled to open in the thirty-six Pussycat Theaters in California. It was what was tastefully referred to as an "erotic film." Amber Hunt, after she finished high school in New York, had been a hairdresser, a cocktail waitress, and then a bunny at the Great Gorge, New York, Playboy Club. She moved to Los Angeles, where she had her picture taken for *Hustler* magazine. When the magazine with Amber's photograph appeared on the newsstands, her boyfriend left her and her father, a New York policeman, wrote her to say she was no longer welcome at home.

A reporter talked to her about her career and the filming of *Cry for Cindy:* "I'm not going to put myself on a pedestal and say I'm the greatest actress in the world," she said, "but I have potential. I'll get very good. I just don't want people to come see me fuck. I want them to come see me act. I'm an actress. It was hard work, but it was more difficult for the actors. With the director screaming at you, it was hard for the men to keep an erection."

Joan Hitchcock said simply, "I didn't know what kind

of film they were making. They just rented my house."
Joan was forty-two and did not need to depend on
Amber Hunt or her own slightly sagging chest for attention; she had a claim to national celebrity. She announced to the press that she had gone to bed with John
Fitzgerald Kennedy, "I think I was number one hundred
and two," she said proudly.

Even Angelina Alioto achieved celebrity. When her
husband was elected mayor of San Francisco in 1967,
Angelina assumed she would automatically be granted
entry into the Golden Circle. She was wrong. Her invitations were politely declined by the inner circle, and she
was quietly but firmly regarded as a social climber.

This infuriated Angelina. She bought all her clothes in
Paris and amassed an enormously expensive collection of
jewelry—after all, she was the wife of the mayor. She
icily informed the press that it was about time she had a
box at the opera; a box at the opera was quickly assigned
to her. Then she told the press that her native Dallas
was more sophisticated than San Francisco. She said San
Francisco was provincial. She went out of her way to
make sure the society editors noticed her.

When the city of San Francisco gave an official banquet for Olav V, the king of Norway, in the marble
rotunda of the City Hall, Mrs. Alioto was seated next to
the king. The press was officially banned from the
banquet, but the society editor of the *Chronicle* was
recognized in the back of the room. Mrs. Alioto gestured
to her and signaled her to come to the head table. She
hesitantly approached. Mrs. Alioto interrupted the king
of Norway and pointed to the society editor. "King," she
said, "this is Miss Moffat. Miss Moffat, this is the king."

But this was not how Angelina became a celebrity.

267

Her husband was reelected in 1971, and in early 1974, feeling he was sufficiently popular to announce that he was a candidate for the democratic nomination for governor of California, he began campaigning throughout California.

When the campaign was in full swing, the headlines in the *Chronicle* announced that Angelina Alioto had disappeared. A statewide search was mounted under the direction of the mayor. The search combed every part of the state, attracting headlines throughout the nation. Then, Angelina suddenly reappeared in Santa Cruz. She had been, she said, making a tour of the California missions.

At a jammed press conference, Angelina was, for once, the star. While her husband listened, she explained he had been ignoring her. He hadn't even asked her thoughts when he decided to run for governor. He had taken her for granted. He had treated her like dirt.

Mayor Alioto smiled bravely. When Angelina finished castigating him, he proudly announced that only in a truly modern and liberated household could a wife make her husband look like an idiot on nationwide television. He hinted that such a couple was what California needed in the statehouse. You had to admire his nerve. Cameras carried pictures of the couple to every part of the nation and the press conference was reported in every major newspaper. Mayor Alioto lost the election, and Angelina announced she wanted a divorce.

It was hard to get excited about what a San Francisco socialite wore to a wedding when television, *People* magazine and the *National Enquirer* could tell you the most intimate details about the sex life of a president or the contents of the secretary of state's garbage can. Electronic media created a whole new gallery of national and international celebrities; if you read the newspapers and magazines, you knew more about the personal lives of the Kennedys than you knew about your own next door neighbor. Nothing was sacred. Photographers fought for pictures of Jacqueline Kennedy Onassis eating, sunbathing or falling off a horse.

There were no more delicious local stories about the parties one-time jetset queen Pat Montundan used to give. Pat was caught up with women's rights and kept her maiden name, even after marrying multimillionaire Alfred Wilsey. Now, she gave consciousness-raising lunches at which everyone talked of rape, saving the whales and how to deprogram children snared by the Hare Krishnas or the Reverend Sun Myung Moon.

Photographers swarmed outside a London town house in November 1975, to photograph the guests leaving an extremely posh party given by Lord and Lady Lambton. Andy Warhol appeared. Then rock music star Keith Moon and Bianca Jagger, the wife of Mick Jagger, another rock star. Finally, the person the photographers were waiting for came out: Caroline Kennedy, the daughter of John Fitzgerald Kennedy. Her hair was frizzy and her eyes were heavily made up. She was seventeen. She was escorted by an enormous young man with curly black hair wearing a black-trimmed white evening jacket. The reporters identified him as Thomas Alexander Fermor-Hesketh, the third baron of Hesketh, "stately homeowner, motor racing sponsor, and one of England's most eligible bachelors." He was twenty-five.

Fermor-Hesketh was none other than the great grandson of Thomas Fermor-Hesketh, "the best specimen of thoroughbred Englishman ever to visit California," who had wooed and won Flora Sharon in the elevator of the Palace Hotel in 1880.

The young Alexander had become the idol of the jetset, flying wherever it was fashionable to fly and leaving the instant the excitement began to falter. One day in 1973, he appeared in San Francisco, dressed in a silk shirt and blazer bearing the family crest, to make what he called a "vast and fabulous deal" with Standard Oil which was anxious to buy a corner of Scotland he owned. He was everywhere: he was having lunch with Truman Capote; he was visiting cabarets around town; he was arriving at the grand opening of Vidal Sassoon's new hair salon on Grant Avenue. As he stepped from his limousine onto the red carpet, Vidal Sassoon himself shook his hand. "Vidal," someone said. "This is Lord Hesketh." "Nice to meet you, Lloyd," Sassoon said.

Then he was describing his new one-hundred-and-fifteen-foot yacht to the press, "I'm naming her 'the Cuddles,'" he said. That was his nickname for his mother, Lady Hesketh. "The crew of six will wear T-shirts with 'Cuddles' across the front, while I stand on the bridge wearing the uniform of an admiral in the Russian Navy. No, not the Imperial Russian Navy, the Communist Navy—big red star and all. I shall be wearing it when I steam into St. Francis Yacht Harbor to shake up the natives who, so far as I can see, need a good shaking up." This pronouncement made, Lord Hesketh hurried off to catch a plane to another fashionable and fast-moving place in the world.

Young Hesketh belonged to his ancestors' era of conspicuous consumption, as did another scion of the Golden Circle, Charles Elkins, who was wooing an attractive Swedish girl named Eva. He flew to Los Angeles and invited her to lunch. Elkin's chauffeured limousine drove them to the Los Angeles Coliseum, where a special gate was prepared to open. The car drove into the center of the vast, empty arena. The couple got out of the car and the chauffeur laid out an elegant picnic basket, crystal stemware and a bottle of wine. They lunched in the middle of the empty stadium. When they finished, Elkins told Eva to look at the scoreboard. She did and lights flashed, "Eva, I love you. Will you marry me?"

That is the kind of story shop girls love to read about high society. Now, they never read about the Crockers. Few are left in San Francisco and none in the Crocker Bank. Charles Crocker III keeps a low profile. His successful investment firm handles, among other projects, an amusement park in the Mother Lode where the Sierra Railroad takes city dwellers and suburbians' children for rides on steam trains. Young Crocker, a true descendant of the railroad tycoon, has one of the largest collection of steam locomotives in the country and frequently rents them to movie companies making westerns.

Charles Crocker and his wife Lucinda have a country home in Napa Valley. Sometimes they give house parties in the mansion his father, Dr. Charles Crocker, built along the 17-Mile-Drive in Pebble Beach. For other old families, Tahoe is the last resort. Families with homes along the Gold Coast of this mile-high lake find security in wearing their grandparents' clothes and cruising in their great-uncle's boats. They fill their houses with Indian artifacts and ancient wicker furniture. When not complaining about taxes, they spend all their time entertaining each other. The pecking order starts with Mrs. Robert Watt Miller, the Folger heiress, who treats innumerable grandchildren to holidays at the lake, while she sets up a calendar of luncheons and dinners. All hands entertain the same people—plus weekend guests—during the month of August, the *in* month at Tahoe. Then tanned, but exhausted, they return to San Francisco for the opera opening.

Vacations are less of a ritual for the new open-ended society. They are involved with causes: saving the whales, prison reform and support for COYOTE (Call Off Your Tired Old Ethics), an organization started in 1973 by a former prostitute, Margo St. James. Its aim is to unite hookers and protect them from police harassment while the "johns" go free. Out of COYOTE grew the annual Hookers Ball, which is attended by an eclectic group of merrymakers which caused Sally Stanford, once the madam of the city's grandest bordello, to congratulate herself on going straight after World War II. Sally bought a restaurant in Sausalito and plunged into politics. She ran for city council so many times she was finally elected by sheer exposure. Then she became mayor.

What's left of society is always trying to think of new ideas for benefits. Money must be raised for culture, hospitals and diseases. Mrs. John Ward Mailliard III is the ringleader of these events. The energetic blond's most unusual venture of the mid-1970's was an attempt to form a new San Francisco historical society.

"We wanted to get away from the stuffiness of other historical societies," said the former Miss Texas, now the wife of a Napoleonic Mailliard. "We looked around for a place for the party and found a real kinky one in North Beach." The organization of the new historical society never got off the ground, but Charlotte rallied her crowd to learn the new dance steps, the Hustle and the Bump, at a sleazy disco called "Dance Your Ass Off."

BIBLIOGRAPHY

ALTROCCHI, JULIA. *The Spectacular San Franciscans.* New York: E.P. Dutton, 1949.

AMERICAN GUIDE SERIES. *San Francisco, Its Bay and Its Cities.* New York: Hastings House, 1947.

AMORY, CLEVELAND. *Who Killed Society?* New York: Harper & Brothers, 1960.

ATHERTON, GERTRUDE. *California, an Intimate History.* New York: Harper & Brothers, 1914.

———. *Adventures of a Novelist.* New York: Liveright, 1932.

BRONSON, WILLIAM. *The Earth Shook, the Sky Burned.* Garden City, New York: Doubleday & Company, 1959.

CAEN, HERB. *Don't Call It Frisco.* Garden City, New York: Doubleday & Company, 1953.

273

————. *One Man's San Francisco.* Garden City, New York: Doubleday & Company, 1976.

CASE, ALEXANDER T. *The Annals of the Bohemian Club.* San Francisco: Recorder-Sunset Press, 1972.

CHAMBLISS, WILLIAM H. *Society as It Really Is.* New York: Chambliss & Company, 1895.

CROCKER, AIMEE. *And I'd Do It Again.* New York: Coward, McCann, Inc., 1936.

DICKSON, SAMUEL. *Tales of San Francisco.* Stanford, California: Stanford University Press, 1947.

DILLON, RICHARD. *Fool's Gold.* New York: Coward, McCann, Inc., 1967.

DOBIE, CHARLES CALDWELL. *San Francisco—A Pageant.* New York: D. Appleton Company, 1934.

GAGEY, EDMOND M. *The San Francisco Stage.* New York: Columbia University Press, 1950.

GEARY, JOHN W. *Diary.* Rare Books Collection, San Francisco Public Library.

GENTRY, CURT. *The Madams of San Francisco.* Garden City, New York: Doubleday & Company, 1964.

HOLDREDGE, HELEN. *Firebelle Lillie.* New York: Meredith Press, 1967.

KRONINGER, ROBERT H. *Sarah and the Senator.* New York: Howell-North Books, 1964.

LAPHAM, HELEN ABBOT. *Roving with Roger.* San Francisco: James A. Barry Company, 1970.

BIBLIOGRAPHY

LAVENDER, DAVID. *The Great Persuader.* Garden City, New York: Doubleday & Company, 1970.

LEWIS, OSCAR. *Big Four.* New York: Alfred A. Knopf, 1938.

———. *Silver Kings.* New York: Alfred A. Knopf, 1947.

LEWIS, OSCAR, AND CARROLL HALL. *Bonanza Inn.* New York: Alfred A. Knopf, 1939.

MCDOUGALL, RUTH BRANSTEN. *Under Mannie's Hat.* San Francisco: Fay L. Frisco Company, 1964.

NEVILLE, AMELIA RANSOME. *Fantastic City.* Boston: Houghton Mifflin Company, 1932.

NEWHALL, RUTH. *The Folger Way.* San Francisco: J. A. Folger & Company.

OLDER, MRS. FREMONT. *San Francisco Magic City.* London: Longmans, Green & Company, 1961.

RATHER, LOIS. *Jessie Fremont at Black Point.* Hand-set, printed and bound by Clif and Lois Rather.

ROBBINS, MILDRED BROWN. *Tales of Love and Hate in San Francisco.* San Francisco: Chronicle Books, 1971.

RODMAN, PAUL. *The California Gold Discovery.* San Francisco: Talisman Press, 1966.

SIEFKIN, DAVID. *The City at the End of the Rainbow.* New York: G.P. Putnam's Sons, 1976.

SOULE, FRANK. *The Annals of San Francisco.* San Francisco: D. Appleton & Company, 1855.

STONE, IRVING. *Men to Match My Mountains.* Garden City, New York: Doubleday & Company, 1956.

TAPER, BERNARD. *Mark Twain's San Francisco.* New York: McGraw-Hill Book Company, 1963.

TEISER, RUTH. *This Sudden Empire.* San Francisco: Taylor and Taylor, 1950.

THARP, LOUISE HALL. *Three Saints and a Sinner.* Boston: Little, Brown & Company, 1956.

THOMAS, LATELY. *Debonair Scoundrel.* New York: Holt, Rinehart and Winston, Inc., 1962.

————. *Sam Ward, King of the Lobby.* Boston: Houghton Mifflin Company, 1965.

————. *Between Two Empires.* Boston: Houghton Mifflin Company, 1969.

TREADWELL, EDWARD F. *Cattle King.* New York: Macmillan Company, 1931.

WELLS, EVELYN. *Champagne Days of San Francisco.* New York: D. Appleton-Century Company, 1941.

INDEX